POPULAR MECHANICS

HOME HOW-TO

HOME REPAIRS and IMPROVEMENTS

ALBERT JACKSON & DAVID DAY

HEARST BOOKS

This work has been extracted from *Popular Mechanics Home How-To*
published by Hearst Books
and created exclusively for William Collins Sons & Co. Ltd. by
Jackson Day Jennings Ltd
trading as Inklink.

Please note:
Great care has been taken to ensure the accuracy of the information in this
book. However, in view of the complex and changing nature of building
regulations, codes, and by-laws, the authors and publishers advise consultation
with specialists in appropriate instances and cannot assume responsibility for
any loss or damage resulting from reliance solely upon the information herein.

Library of Congress Cataloging-in-Publication Data

Jackson, Albert, 1943–
 Popular mechanics home how-to. Home repairs and improvements /
Albert Jackson and David Day.
  p. cm.
 Includes index.
 ISBN 1-58816-075-0
 1. Dwellings—Maintenance and repair—Amateurs' manuals. I. Title:
Home repairs and improvements. II. Day, David, 1944– III. Title.

TH48917.3 J33 2002
643'.7—dc21   2001039116

Printed in Spain

Second Edition

1 2 3 4 5 6 7 8 9 10

CONTENTS

HOW TO USE THIS BOOK

This book has been written and designed to make finding information as easy as possible. **Running heads** identify the subjects covered on each page. **Tinted boxes** separate and highlight information related to the main text. **Headings** divide the main text into subsections so that you can easily locate specific information or a single stage in the work. **Cross-references** direct you to related information elsewhere in the book. The symbol ▷ next to a word indicates that the subject is discussed on another page. The specific cross-reference is listed in the margin of the page you're on. Cross-references printed in bold type are directly related to the task at hand. Those printed in lighter type will broaden your understanding of the subject.

HOUSE CONSTRUCTION: FRAME

Wood is the predominant material used in residential construction for both structural and finish applications. While there are several approaches to framing a structure with wood, the platform framing system, illustrated at the right, is most widely used.

Foundations

The foundations for frame houses are generally poured concrete or concrete block. Footings should be present under all perimeter walls and beneath any loadbearing walls or columns.

Floor construction

In platform framing, the first-floor structure is fastened to sill plates that rest on top of the foundation walls. The basic floor structure is made from 2-inch-thick joists. The ends of joists are joined to joist headers, and cross-braces are nailed between joists to prevent twisting. Where openings occur in the joist pattern for stairways or other passages through the floor plane, doubled headers and doubled joists along the sides of the opening are added. Subflooring and finish flooring are applied over the floor frame.

Wall construction

The walls of frame houses are ordinarily built by fastening studs to horizontal members called top and toe plates (◁). The wall frames are fastened to the floor frames. Loadbearing walls have a doubled top plate. Where the ordinary stud spacing pattern is interrupted for window and door openings in bearing walls, special headers are fashioned to support the weight above each opening.

In another framing approach called "balloon framing," wall studs rise from the first floor to the top floor ceiling structure, and intermediate floor frames are attached to the wall studs.

The exterior wall frames are covered with sheathing, and then building paper is applied before the wall finish is added.

Roof structure

In simple pitched roofs, rafters rest on top of house walls and join to a ridge board at the peak. The roof deck is formed by fastening sheathing over the structural members, and is then covered with asphalt felt, which is in turn finished with asphalt or wood shingles. Slate and clay tile finishes are also common.

Foundations
The foundation carries the whole weight of the house. The type, size and depth are determined largely by the loadbearing properties of the subsoil.

Strip foundation
A continuous strip of concrete set well below ground.

Slab on footings
Houses without basements or crawlspaces may have this type of foundation. In cold climates footing must be set deep enough to fall below the frostline.

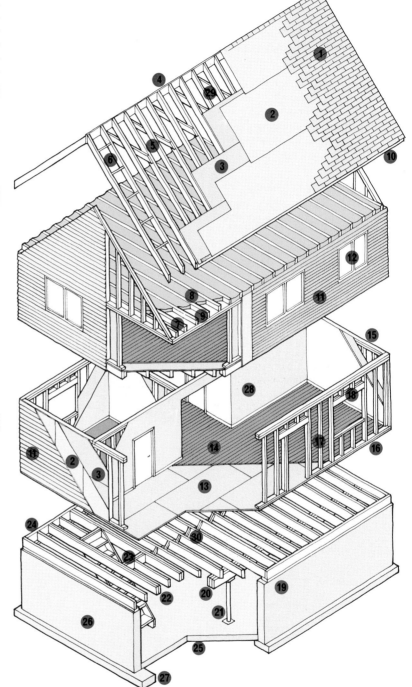

TYPICAL COMPONENTS OF A FRAME HOUSE

1 Asphalt shingles	9 Vapor barrier	17 Stud	24 Joist header
2 Asphalt felt	10 Fascia	18 Header	25 Concrete slab
3 Sheathing	11 Siding	19 Sill plate	26 Foundation wall
4 Ridge board	12 Window unit	20 Girder	27 Footing
5 Rafters	13 Subflooring	21 Column	28 Loadbearing
6 Lookouts	14 Finish flooring	22 Doubled joist	partition
7 Joists	15 Doubled top plate	23 Doubled joist	29 Collar beam
8 Insulation	16 Toe plate	header	30 Cross-bracing

BRICK HOUSE CONSTRUCTION

While a brick veneer may confer a degree of nobility to a frame house, a true brick house is, to many, the essence of solidity and permanence. Typical construction details for brick houses are illustrated at the left.

Foundation

Brick houses generally have a deep, strip-type foundation of block or concrete. In older houses, stone or brick may have been used to build foundation walls.

Wall structure

Cavity wall construction is used to build the perimeter walls of most brick houses—each wall consists of an inner and outer leaf separated by an airspace (▷). The two leaves are braced with metal or brick ties. A flashing just above ground level keeps dampness from the ground from migrating up the walls. Rigid insulation is often placed in the airspace.

For economy, especially in more recently built homes, concrete blocks are frequently used for the inner wall, and the interior surface is generally finished with plaster. Interior partitions are generally framed with wood studs over which wood or wire lath is placed to hold the plaster finish. In large apartment buildings built prior to World War II, you may find gypsum block partitions finished with plaster.

For structural purposes, the tops of door and window openings in brick walls are treated with lintels of stone, steel or precast concrete. Brick arches are a decorative alternative to lintels.

Floor structure

The ends of floor joists generally rest on recesses in the brick walls. Cross-bracing is used between them and they may be supported between perimeter walls with columns or girders. As in frame houses, subflooring is applied over joists, and the finish flooring is installed over the subfloor.

Roof structure

In many brick houses, the roof structure is similar to that used in frame houses, but if the roof finish is slate or tile, the structure must be reinforced with purlins or trusses to support the additional weight.

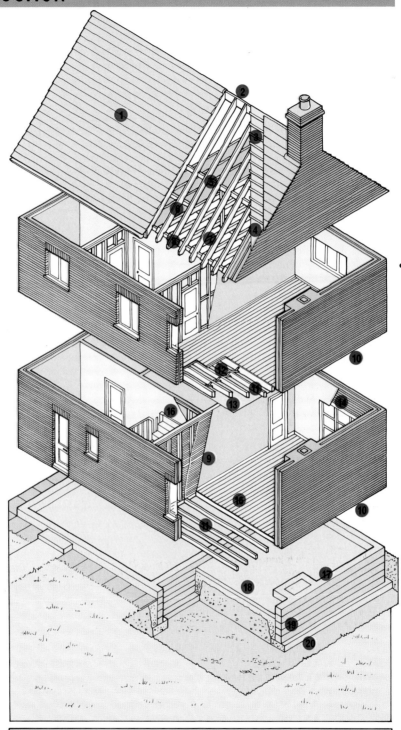

● **Foundation problems**
Consult a professional engineer or architect when dealing with problems or new work involving foundations.

Settlement
Settlement cracks in walls are not uncommon. If they are not too wide and have stabilized, they are not a serious problem.

Subsidence
Subsidence caused by weak or shallow foundations or excessive moisture-loss from the ground—can be more serious. Widening cracks from window or door openings indicate this.

Heave
Weak foundations can also be damaged by ground swell, or "heave."

Light foundations
The walls of extensions or bays with lighter or shallower foundations than the house may show cracks where the two meet due to differential movement.

TYPICAL COMPONENTS OF A BRICK HOUSE

1 Tile or slate	9 Lath-and-plaster	16 Finish flooring
2 Ridge board	stud partition	17 Flashing
3 Nailers	10 Brick cavity wall	18 Concrete slab
4 Asphalt felt	11 Floor joists	19 Foundation wall
5 Purlin	12 Cross-bracing	20 Footing
6 Rafter	13 Plaster ceiling	
7 Ceiling joist	14 Lintel	
8 Wall plate	15 Staircase	

WALLS: EXTERIOR WALLS

Exterior walls are built to bear the structural loads of the house, to keep out weather and unwanted noises, to trap heat and to serve as a decorative element in the

home's design. There are numerous structural approaches for exterior walls; the most common ones are illustrated and described below.

Wall ties
Wall ties are laid in the mortar joints and bridge the airspace between the inner and outer leaves. In brick veneer walls, the ties are fastened to the sheathing.

Wire butterfly tie

Sheet metal tie

Frame wall construction

In wood frame houses, exterior walls are usually built with 2-by-4 studs nailed 16 inches on center to top and toe plates, and since exterior walls carry much of the structural load, wall top plates are doubled.

Sheathing is nailed to the outer surface of the wall frame to add rigidity, and is then covered with a weather-resistant membrane. Wood, plywood, hardboard, vinyl and aluminum sidings are nailed directly to the membrane-covered sheathing. When the exterior finish is made of brick or stucco veneer, there is generally a 1-inch airspace between the sheathing and veneer.

Fiberglass batt or mineral fiber insulation is frequently used in the stud cavities. A vapor barrier is applied to the interior edges of the wall frame before attaching the interior wall finish—gypsum wallboard, plaster or paneling.

Masonry construction

Very old stone houses may be built with solid walls, but in most masonry construction, cavity walls, consisting of an inner and outer leaf separated by an airspace, are the norm. The two leaves are braced with wall ties running between them, which are then set in the mortar joints. In modern masonry construction, rigid insulation may be set in the airspace, and cement block instead of brick may be used for the inner leaf for economy.

Exterior wall construction
1 Frame wall with wood siding
2 Frame wall with brick veneer
3 Brick cavity wall
4 Frame wall with stucco veneer
5 Brick cavity wall with block inner leaf
6 Solid stone wall

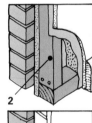 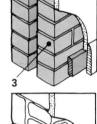 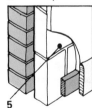 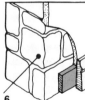

Superinsulated frame walls

Superinsulated frame wall

In recent years, new approaches to wall framing and insulation have been developed in the interest of conserving energy. Typical of various super-insulation approaches has been the use of 2-by-6 studs and plates to create deeper stud cavities that permit the installation of thicker insulation. The added insulation significantly improves the R-value of house walls, a standard that measures structural resistance to the passage of thermal energy.

In addition to improving R-values with thicker insulation and insulated sheathing materials, superinsulating techniques also protect insulation from moisture damage and reduce air infiltration through seams and joints by special attention to the application of the vapor barrier. The vapor barrier is carefully wrapped around corners and at floor and ceiling joints, and the wall finish is often spaced away from the barrier with furring to prevent its being torn by fasteners. The vapor barrier is also carefully sealed around electrical boxes and other mechanical fixtures. Semi-permeable housewraps have been developed for the membrane between the sheathing and siding; these permit moisture to escape from the wall cavity but screen out drafts.

IDENTIFYING LOADBEARING WALLS

When appraising the condition of a house or planning a remodeling project, distinguishing between loadbearing and non-loadbearing walls is critical (◁). In general, the exterior walls of a house are loadbearing, that is, they transmit the weight of the roof and floor loads of upper stories to the foundation. If you took the finish off exterior walls, you would find that they utilize special structural elements—frame walls have doubled top plates and broad doubled headers over window and door openings where the normal stud-spacing pattern is interrupted to bear the weight above. If, when you inspect a house, exterior walls appear to buckle, show unusual cracks or vertical or horizontal misalignment, it is evidence of a severe structural problem. And if you altered the structural scheme of an existing exterior wall to build an addition to a home, you would have to design an alternative means of supporting the loads formerly borne by the altered wall.

Interior walls may be loadbearing or non-loadbearing. If a wall runs parallel to floor joists, chances are it has no structural purpose other than to divide the interior space. But if a wall runs perpendicular to joists and you find a similar wall or lollicolumns aligned directly below the wall on a lower story, the wall is loadbearing. A loadbearing wall may also rest on a girder, that is, a heavy horizontal member of steel or wood. Like exterior loadbearing walls, interior bearing walls cannot be removed or structurally altered without providing support for related elements of the building. Obtain advice from a professional architect or engineer before proceeding with alterations to loadbearing walls (◁).

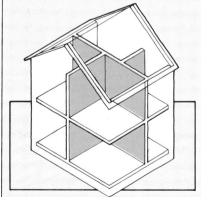

Non-loadbearing walls
These walls divide internal space into rooms and could be removed without damaging the structure.

INTERIOR WALLS

The type of interior wall construction and finish will depend to a certain extent on the age of the building and on the function of the wall within the structure. The most common types are illustrated and discussed on this page.

Wood frame walls

Wood framing is by far the most common structural system used for both interior loadbearing and non-loadbearing partitions (▷). Specific structural differences between the two may consist only of a doubled top plate and more extensive cross-bracing in loadbearing walls. In general, wall studs are set 16 inches on center apart and nailed to top and toe plates. In some non-structural walls, wall studs are set 24 inches on center.

In older houses, thin, closely-spaced wood lath strips are nailed to the wall frame to serve as a structural basis for plaster. Plaster is frequently applied in two coats—an undercoat of brown plaster followed by a finish coat of white finish plaster (▷). In newer buildings,

metal wire lath is used as the structural ground for plaster instead of wood lath. Metal lath over wood studs is also frequently found where the wall finish is ceramic tile set over concrete plaster.

In the vast majority of homes built after World War II, interior walls are wood frame finished with gypsum wallboard. The wallboard is nailed to the wall frame in sheets, and seams are finished with a cellulose-base wallboard compound. In some cases, a gypsum product similar to wallboard is nailed to the wall frame and finished with a skim-coat of plaster. Where ceramic tile is applied over a wallboard finish, a mastic adhesive is used as the bonding agent.

Metal stud walls

In recent years, metal stud systems have increasingly been used to construct interior partitions for economy and because of their fire resistance (▷). It is likely that those living in apartment buildings constructed after 1970 will find partitions framed with metal studs and finished with gypsum wallboard, which is fastened to the framing with

special screws.

Metal studs and the track that is used for top and toe plates are nominally U-shaped. These materials are easily cut with tin snips or aviation shears. Studs are crimped into place in the tracks, which are used for top and toe plates, and are ordinarily easy to remove with a firm twist.

Non-frame walls

In some masonry buildings, especially large apartment buildings constructed between 1890 and 1945, interior partions may be constructed with lightweight gypsum block or hollow clay block. In most cases with this type of interior wall construction, the wall finish is plaster applied directly to the block. While it is advisable to check with a professional before removing any wall or cutting an opening in it, hollow-block partitions are, in most cases, non-loadbearing. After ascertaining that such a wall serves no critical structural purpose, you can easily break down or open hollow block walls with a sledge hammer and cold chisel. The top of openings in block walls will require a lintel for support (▷).

In modern construction, concrete block walls are frequently used as party walls to separate attached housing units. The wall finish may be plaster or gypsum

wallboard. Concrete-block walls are designed to contain the spread of fires and also provide good sound insulation. Generally speaking, party walls are structural and should not be altered without obtaining professional advice and legal permission.

In the most advanced building technology that's being increasingly applied in factory-built, modular homes, walls consist of "stressed-skin panels." While many of the systems are proprietary and the terminology is not entirely uniform, the term usually refers to a wall system that is made with an inner core of rigid foam to which plywood, particleboard or gypsum wallboard has been laminated. The panels have interlocking joints. Never alter a stressed-skin panel structure without consulting the manufacturer for the correct procedure and specifications.

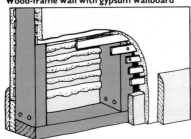

Wood-frame wall with gypsum wallboard

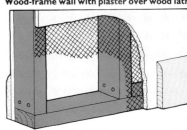

Wood-frame wall with plaster over wood lath

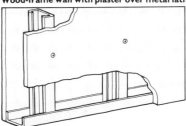

Wood-frame wall with plaster over metal lath

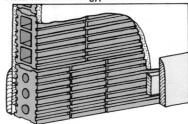

Metal stud wall with gypsum wallboard

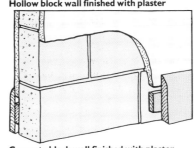

Hollow block wall finished with plaster

Concrete block wall finished with plaster

SEE ALSO	
Details for:▷	
Spanning wall openings	8
Stud partitions	20-23
Metal studs	24-25
Plasterwork	32-39

Glass blocks
Hollow glass blocks can be used for non-loadbearing walls. Made in square and rectangular shapes and a range of colors they can be laid in mortar or dry-set with plastic jointing strips in a frame.

SEE ALSO
◁Details for:
Opening masonry walls 14-15

TYPES OF LINTELS

A lintel is used in brick, block and stone construction to bridge a gap above a window, door or other wall opening.

WOOD AND STEEL

In frame buildings with a brick veneer, a rolled-steel angle is frequently used to support the brick above a door or window opening. The lintel, however, does little to support the overall roof and wall structure. Instead, a wood header whose dimensions are based on the load and span of the opening is installed behind the steel lintel.

FLAT ROLLED STEEL

A flat rolled-steel lintel is sometimes used to support a soldier course of brick to form a lintel. This lintel construction method is not especially strong and is generally limited to brick veneer structures.

REINFORCED CONCRETE

Precast concrete lintels are among the most widely used in modern masonry construction. While concrete bears compression loads well, it does not resist tension well. Because lintels are subject to both types of forces, precast concrete lintels have steel reinforcing bars embedded in them to improve their tensile strength.

Prestressed concrete lintels, reinforced with wire strands set in the concrete under tension, are lighter than other concrete lintels. Precast concrete lintels are available in a variety of standard sizes to match wall thicknesses and course heights, but may be rather awkward to handle in large sizes. Some concrete lintels are cast with a hollow that is reinforced with steel and filled with grout after being set in place.

ROLLED-STEEL ANGLES

Rolled-steel angles are commonly used for lintels in masonry construction; the size of the angle is based on the load. Inserting an angle at the top of the opening in each leaf of a cavity wall is on standard method, but sometimes angles are bolted together or welded to other steel members of the building's structural frame.

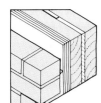
Stone and timber

Brick and steel

Reinforced concrete

Pressed steel

Rolled steel

SPANNING OPENINGS IN BRICK WALLS

Creating an opening in a brick or block wall for a door or window requires installation of a lintel to support the structural load above it. Some structural principles relating to brick walls are discussed below.

Where supports are needed

Door or window frames aren't designed to carry superimposed loads, so the load from floors above—even the brickwork above the opening—must be supported by a rigid beam called a lintel, which transmits the weight to the sides where the bearings are firm. Wider openings call for stronger beams, such as rolled-steel lintels. There are numerous beams, but all work in the same way.

The forces on a beam

When a load is placed at the center of a beam supported at each end, the beam will bend. The lower portion is being stretched and is in "tension;" the top portion is being squeezed and is in "compression." The beam is also subjected to "shear" forces where the vertical load is trying to sever the beam at the points of support. A beam must be able to resist these forces. This is achieved by the correct choice of material and the depth of the beam in relation to the imposed load and the span of the opening.

Calculating lintel size

The purpose of a lintel is to form a straight bridge across an opening, which can carry the load of the structure above it. The load may be relatively light, being no more than a number of brick or block courses. It is more likely that other loads from upper floors and the roof will also bear on the lintel.

The size of the lintel must be suitable for the job it has to do. The size should be derived from calculations based on the weight of the materials used in the construction of the building. Calculation for specifying a beam is a job for an architect or structural engineer. Tables relating to the weight of the materials are used on which to base the figures.

In practice, for typical situations, a builder can help you decide on the required size of lintel based on his experience. A building inspector usually will be happy to accept this type of specification, but he can insist that proper calculations are also submitted along with your application for a building permit.

When to support a wall

If you are creating a door, window or finished opening which is no wider than 3 feet across in a non-loadbearing wall, you can cut the hole without having to support the wall above providing the wall is properly bonded and sound. The only area of brickwork that is likely to collapse is roughly in the shape of a 45-degree triangle directly above the opening leaving a self-supporting stepped arch of brickwork. This effect is known as "self-corbelling". Do not rely on the self-corbelling effect to support the wall if you plan to make an opening which is more than three feet wide. In that case, temporarily support the wall as if it were loadbearing.

Before you make any opening in a loadbearing wall you will need to erect adjustable props (◁) as temporary supports, not only for the weight of the masonry but also for the loads that bear on it from floors, walls and roof above.

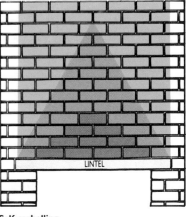
Self-corbelling
The shaded bricks are the only ones at risk of falling out before the lintel is installed because of the self-corbelling effect of the bricks above. Theoretically the lintel supports the weight of the materials within the 60° triangle plus any superimposed floor or roof loading, but when the side walls (piers) are narrow, the load on the lintel is increased to encompass the area of the rectangle.

RIGGING UP ADJUSTABLE PROPS

To remove part of a loadbearing wall it's necessary to temporarily support the wall above the opening. Rent adjustable steel jacks (▷) and scaffold boards to spread the load across the floor. Where part of a bearing wall will remain below the ceiling level, you will also need "needles" to spread the load. Needles can generally be made with 4-by-6 lumber about 6 feet long.

For a window or door opening, probably only one needle and two props will suffice: place the needle centrally over the opening about 6 inches above the lintel or header position. For wider openings, or where a load is great, two needles and four props will be needed, spaced no more than 3 feet apart across the width of the opening.

Cut a hole in the wall for each needle and insert them. Support each end with a prop, which works like a car jack. Stand the props on scaffold boards no more than 2 feet from each side of the wall.

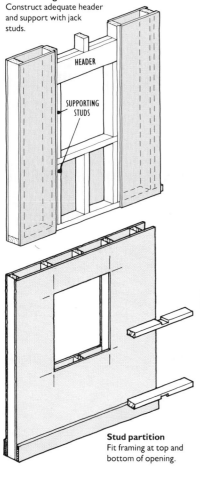

Loadbearing wall
Construct adequate header and support with jack studs.

Stud partition
Fit framing at top and bottom of opening.

MAKING A WALL OPENING

A pass-through is a convenient opening in a wall, usually between a kitchen and dining area, through which you can pass food, drinks and equipment. If you are blocking off a doorway, or making a stud wall, it may be advantageous to allow for a pass-through. You may want to make a pass-through in an existing wall.

Planning the size and shape

Ideally the bottom of the opening should be an extension of the kitchen worktop or at least flush with a work surface: 3 feet is a comfortable working height and the standard height for kitchen worktops. For practicality—passing through a tray and serving dishes, for instance—it should not be narrower than 2 feet 6 inches.

Hatches should be fitted with some means of closing the opening for privacy, preventing cooking odors from drifting and, in some cases, as a fire-check (see right).

Creating the opening in a masonry wall

You can make an opening in either a loadbearing or a solid non-loadbearing wall in much the same way: the main requirement with the former is temporarily supporting the structure above and the load imposed on the wall (▷). Mark the position for the opening on one side of the wall. Align the hole with the vertical and horizontal mortar courses between bricks or blocks to save having to cut too many bricks—break away a square of plaster at the center to locate the joints.

Mark out the shape and position of the opening on the other side of the wall using adjacent walls, the ceiling and floor as references, or drill through at the corners. Make the hole about 1 inch oversize to allow for a jamb. Mark the lintel position.

Set up adjustable props and needles if you're working on a loadbearing wall (see left), then chop a slot for the lintel with a sledgehammer and bolster chisel—on a brick wall this will probably be a single course of bricks deep; on a block wall, remove a whole course of blocks and fill the gap with bricks. Trowel mortar onto the bearings and set the lintel in place. Use a level to check that the lintel is perfectly horizontal—pack under it with pieces of slate if necessary. Replace any bricks above the lintel that have dropped. Leave 24 hours to set, then remove props, needles and the masonry below.

Making an opening in a stud wall

Cutting an opening in a non-loadbearing stud partition wall is simpler than making one in a solid wall, but if the wall bears some weight you'll need to support the floor or ceiling above with props using planks to spread the load.

Mark out, then cut away the wallboard or lath-and-plaster covering from each side to expose the studs. For an opening the width between studs (16 inches), just toenail 2-by-4s between them at the top and bottom of the opening. If it will be wider, make the opening span three studs. Cut away part of the middle stud at the height you want the jamb, allowing for the thickness of a horizontal frame member above and below the opening. Make the framing from 2-by-4 lumber and cut them to fit between the two studs on each side of the cut one. Fit and check for level.

Fitting a finished jamb

Line the four sides of the opening with ¾-inch-thick pine of a width equal to the wall thickness joined at the corners with butt joints or 45-degree miter joints for a neater result. The frame can finish flush with the wall surface and be covered with a casing, or project beyond the wall finish to form a lip.

The sides of the opening in a masonry wall may be rough—it's not easy to cut a clean line. Make and fit the frame, then shim out the gap between masonry and lining with wood shingles—the frame must be square within the opening; check with a level. Screw the frame to masonry with lead anchors, fitted when the frame is positioned. Fill gaps with mortar. Rake back the surface of the mortar. When set finish flush with plaster.

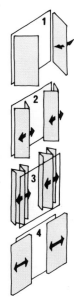

Pass-through doors
1 Double-hinged
2 Twin bi-fold
3 Concertina
4 Horizontal-sliding

Finishing the frame
Use a casing to cover the joint between the jamb and wall or let the frame project to mask it.

Fit a casing

Let jamb project

9

CUTTING AN INTERIOR DOORWAY

In an interior remodeling project, you may wish to create a doorway in an existing solid wall. First determine whether the wall is loadbearing or non-loadbearing, *then depending on which is appropriate for your situation, follow one of the procedures explained and illustrated below.*

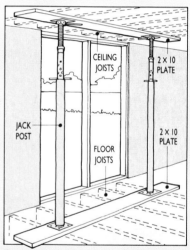

Framing a door opening in a loadbearing wall

You can generally tell whether a wall is loadbearing or nonstructural by removing the wall finish in the area where you wish to situate the door up to the ceiling. Gypsum wallboard can easily be stripped away by cutting with a utility knife or wallboard saw; plaster must be chipped off with a bolster chisel and then the lath must be cut away.

If you find a doubled top plate, you can assume that the wall is loadbearing. A little further checking will probably show floor joists resting on top of the wall frame. This is a clear indication that you will have to set up temporary supports to bear the structural load before removing any wall studs and that you will need to construct a structural header when framing the rough opening for the doorway. Seek professional advice from an engineer or building inspector on specifications for the header. If the opening is 3 feet wide or less, chances are that a wood header of 2-by-12s will be sufficient, but wider openings may require a steel beam.

Place temporary props in place as shown at the right; props must be set on both sides of interior bearing walls. Once adequate support is in place, remove any studs that fall within the area of the desired opening. Cut away the toe plate of the wall from the bottom of the opening.

If it is not convenient to use existing studs as sides for the doorway's rough opening, new studs may be nailed in position as desired. Remember that when setting the width of the rough opening, an allowance must be made for the thickness of the jack studs that will support the structural header and for the materials that will be used to finish its inside edges—either a jamb of ¾-inch thick lumber, plaster or wallboard.

Once the full-length studs at the sides of the rough opening are nailed in place with 10d common nails, nail the jack studs in place. They should be cut to a length equal to the rough opening height. Then nail up the header using 2-inch-thick lumber of the necessary width using scraps of ½-inch-thick plywood as spacers between the two lengths used to make up the header. Set the header in place on top of the jack studs and nail. Insert cripple studs to run from the top of the header to the underside of the doubled top plate—these transmit the structural load to the header.

Once the framing is complete, the temporary props can be removed. The wall finish can be restored, and the door opening can be finished, either with a wood jamb and casing, or with ordinary wall finish materials (◁).

Framing for door opening in a non-loadbearing partition

Framing a door opening in a non-loadbearing partition

A door opening in a nonstructural frame partition is fairly straightforward. The task will be simplest if you can situate the doorway between two existing studs in the wall frame. Start at one end of the wall where you want the opening, and measure off increments of 16 inches to locate the wall studs. Probe the area where you think the studs to be used for sides of the rough jamb are. If you don't find them immediately, measure off 16-inch increments from the opposite end of the wall. If you can't put the opening between two existing studs, you will have to insert new studs to serve as vertical rough jambs.

Draw layout lines on the wall for the sides and top of the opening. The opening will look best if the top aligns with other doors and windows in the room. Remove the baseboard molding, and cut away the wall finish inside the layout lines. At the top of the opening you will have to cut away the wall finish about 2½ inches higher than the layout line. Cut any existing studs that fall within the opening at a point 2½ inches higher than the desired height for the finished opening. (Cut the studs 1½ inches plus the thickness of the wall-finish material higher than the layout mark if you do not plan to install a finished door jamb.) Cut a rough header for the opening from one of the studs you removed and nail it across the top with its wide side down, making sure it is level. Then, install the door jamb or finish the opening as desired.

Alternate door framing methods for non-loadbearing partitions

INSTALLING A STRUCTURAL HEADER

Before you begin to alter the framing of a loadbearing wall to create a doorway or for any reason, it is necessary to set up temporary support. You can rent or purchase adjustable jack posts such as those shown below for this purpose. First, determine the direction of the floor joists and set a length of 2-by-10 lumber on the floor about 2 feet from the wall, perpendicular to the joist direction. Adjust the jack posts to the approximate height needed by setting the pins in the correct holes in the telescoping body. Wedge a second 2-by-10 between the top of the jack posts and the ceiling, setting the jacks plumb. Screw the threaded rod at the top of each jack post upward until the jacks and plates are snug. Make similar setups on both sides of interior walls.

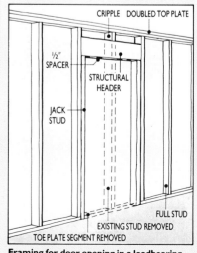

Temporary supports for cutting a door opening

Framing for door opening in a loadbearing wall

FILLING AN OPENING IN A STUD PARTITION

Strip the door jambs as described (see right). Trim the lath-and-plaster or plasterboard back to the center line of the door jamb studs and header, with a sharp utility knife. Remove the old nails with a claw hammer. Nail the new cut edge all around.

Nail a matching toe plate to the floor between the studs. Cut and nail a new stud centrally between header and toe plate. Cut and nail braces between the studs across the opening. Fasten wallboard to each face of the opening. Cut the board 1/8 inch less all around. Fill and tape the joints (▷), then finish as desired with paint or with wallcovering.

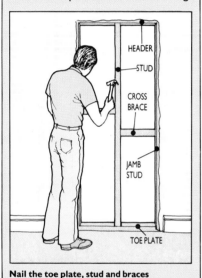

Labels on illustration: HEADER, STUD, CROSS BRACE, JAMB STUD, TOE PLATE

Nail the toe plate, stud and braces

BLOCKING OFF A DOORWAY

If you are making a new opening in a wall, it's possible that you will also have to block off the original one. Obviously, you'll want the patch to be invisible, which takes careful plastering or joint filling of wallboard.

Choosing the right materials

It is better to fill in the opening with the same materials used in the construction of the wall—although you can consider bricks and blocks as the same—to prevent cracks forming from movement in the structure. You could use a wooden stud frame with gypsum lath board and a skimcoat of plaster finish to fill an opening in a brick wall, but it would not have the same acoustic properties as block or brick and cracks are difficult to prevent or disguise.

Removing the woodwork

Saw through the door jambs close to the top and pry them away from the structural framework with a wrecking bar. Start levering at the bottom. If the jambs were fitted before the flooring, the ends could be trapped: cut them flush with the floor. Next, pry the jamb header away from the top.

Bricking up the opening

Cut back the plaster about 6 inches all around the opening. It need not be an even line; unevenness helps to disguise the outline of the doorway.

To bond the new brickwork into the old, cut out a half-brick on each side of the opening at every fourth course, using a sledgehammer and bolster chisel. For a block wall, remove a quarter of a block from alternate courses.

It's not vital to tooth-in the infill if you're using blocks (which are easy and quick to lay) as it will require more cutting to fit. Instead, 4-inch steel cut nails driven dovetail fashion into the bed joints of the side brickwork **(1)** can be used to tie the masonry together.

Galvanized angle brackets can also be used to save cutting into the bricks **(2)**—screw them to the wall, resting on every fourth brick.

Lay the bricks or blocks in mortar, following the original courses. If a wooden suspended floor runs through the opening, lay the bricks on a wood toe plate nailed across the opening. When the mortar has set, spread on a base coat of plaster, followed by a finishing coat (▷). Fit two complete lengths of new matching baseboard, or add to the original. When making up the baseboard from odd pieces, make sure the joints do not occur in the same place as the original opening.

SEE ALSO

Details for:▷	
Plastering a wall	39
Finishing wallboard	46-47

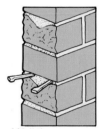

1 Nail ties

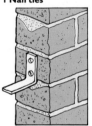

2 Angle bracket tie

Cut out half-bricks

Lay bricks into the courses

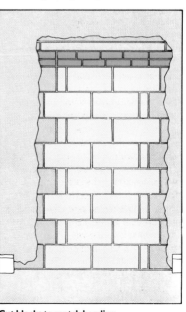

Cut blocks to match bonding

11

CONVERTING TWO ROOMS TO ONE

Removing a wall may be the best way to improve access between areas frequently used—the dining and living rooms, for instance—and of course it can expand your living space considerably. The job uses similar principles to making a pass-through or a new doorway, although on a much larger scale. Removing a dividing wall—whether it's structural or simply a non-loadbearing partition—is a major undertaking, but it need not be overwhelming. If you follow some basic safety and structural rules, much of the job is straightforward, if messy and disruptive. Before you start, plan out your requirements and consult the flow chart, right, for a breakdown of just what's involved.

WHY DO YOU WANT TO REMOVE A WALL?

Before you go ahead and demolish the wall between two rooms, consider just how the new space might function, its appearance, the time it will take you to carry out the work, and the cost.

Ask yourself the following questions:
● Will the shape and size of the new room suit your needs? Remember, if you have a young family, your needs are likely to change as they grow up.
● Will most of the family activities be carried out in the same room (eating, watching TV, playing music, reading, conversation, playing with toys, hobbies, homework)?
● Will removing the wall deprive you of privacy within the family, or from passersby in the street?
● Will the new room feel like one unit and not a conversion? For example, do the baseboards and moldings match?
● Are the fireplaces acceptable when seen together, or should one be removed? Should one of the doorways, if close together, be blocked off?
● Will the loss of a wall make the furniture arrangements difficult—particularly if central-heating radiators are in use and take up valuable wall space elsewhere?
● Will the heating and lighting need to be modified?
● Will the proposed shape of the opening be in character with the room and the right proportion?

● **Hiring professionals**
If you're in doubt, hire a professional builder: to save costs, you may be able to work as a laborer or do preparation and clearing work.

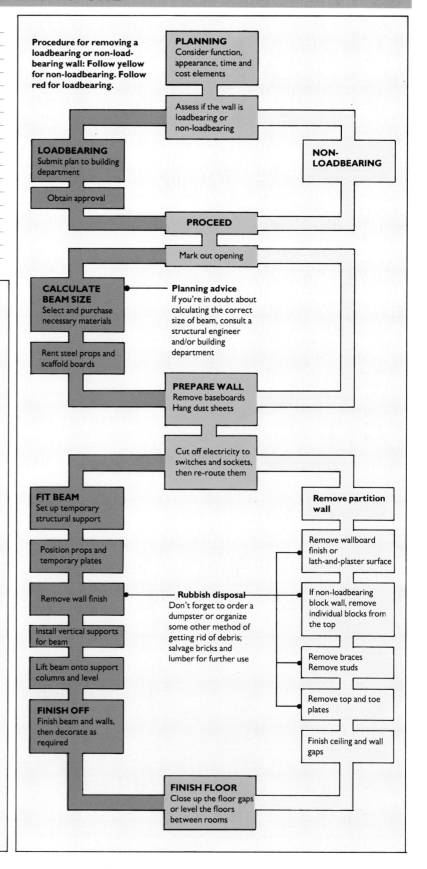

Procedure for removing a loadbearing or non-load-bearing wall: Follow yellow for non-loadbearing. Follow red for loadbearing.

PLANNING
Consider function, appearance, time and cost elements

Assess if the wall is loadbearing or non-loadbearing

LOADBEARING
Submit plan to building department

Obtain approval

NON-LOADBEARING

PROCEED

Mark out opening

CALCULATE BEAM SIZE
Select and purchase necessary materials

Rent steel props and scaffold boards

Planning advice
If you're in doubt about calculating the correct size of beam, consult a structural engineer and/or building department

PREPARE WALL
Remove baseboards
Hang dust sheets

Cut off electricity to switches and sockets, then re-route them

FIT BEAM
Set up temporary structural support

Position props and temporary plates

Remove wall finish

Install vertical supports for beam

Lift beam onto support columns and level

FINISH OFF
Finish beam and walls, then decorate as required

Rubbish disposal
Don't forget to order a dumpster or organize some other method of getting rid of debris; salvage bricks and lumber for further use

Remove partition wall

Remove wallboard finish or lath-and-plaster surface

If non-loadbearing block wall, remove individual blocks from the top

Remove braces
Remove studs

Remove top and toe plates

Finish ceiling and wall gaps

FINISH FLOOR
Close up the floor gaps or level the floors between rooms

If a loadbearing wall is to be removed to create a more open plan, a beam must be installed to maintain the home's structural integrity. The basic concerns of and options for removing a loadbearing wall are discussed below.

Structural concerns

An interior loadbearing wall generally supports the weight of an upper floor and sometimes, depending on the design, part of the weight of the roof. When a loadbearing wall is removed, provisions must be made to support the loads on that wall. Typically, a horizontal beam is installed in the area where joists of the upper floor rested on the top plate of the wall that is being removed. The beam is supported by vertical columns that transmit the load to the foundation and other structural elements of the house frame.

The size of the beam is determined by several factors: the load it must bear, the span between the vertical columns that support it, the distance from the beam to other structural elements that run parallel to it, the material from which the beam is made and local standards for minimum floor load capacities. While determining the necessary size required for a beam in any given situation is a matter for a professional engineer, architect or building official, in general, the greater the load, span between vertical supports, and distance from parallel structural elements, the larger the beam must be. The required thickness and depth of a beam can vary based on variations of the number and spacing of support columns and with the introduction of other structural elements running parallel to the beam.

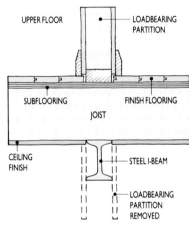

Steel I-beam bears load where structural wall is removed

Choosing a beam

Beams of several different materials can be used to provide structural support where a loadbearing wall is removed. In many cases, rolled steel I-beams are used. Because of steel's great strength, the depth of the beam can be relatively shallow compared with the other options, and this may be an important concern where maximum headroom for an opening is critical. But steel beams can present some difficulties for typical do-it-yourselfers. Most codes require that steel beams be supported by steel columns, and that connections be either welded or bolted—both options require special equipment and skills.

Finishing a steel beam can also be problematic (▷).

Laminated wood-beams are a desirable option preferred by do-it-yourselfers and increasingly specified by architects. The beams are made by laminating several thicknesses of dimension lumber, and several appearance grades are available which may either finished with wallboard or left exposed for decorative effect. Laminated beams can be cut and drilled with ordinary woodworking tools, and can be joined to columns with structural joints, lag screws or approved metal fastening plates.

Planning and approval

It is necessary to obtain a building permit before removing a loadbearing wall. In order to obtain a permit, it is necessary to provide the inspector with drawings that include key details of the existing structure and specifications for the installation of the new supporting structure. While a knowledgeable do-it-yourselfer may be able to prepare such drawings, it is highly recommended that you consult with an architect or structural engineer when tackling a project that involves altering structural elements of a home.

HOW A BEAM IS SUPPORTED

Beams are supported by vertical columns that transmit the load to other structural elements within the building. The required number and spacing of columns is contingent on the load and the size of the beam.

The drawing below illustrates a typical configuration. The structural beam supporting the second floor joists is supported by a column that transmits the weight to the end of a girder notched into the foundation wall. As you move to the left you see another column supporting the beam. That column bears directly on the girder and aligns with a column supporting it. The key point is that columns must align either exactly or very nearly to maintain the structural integrity of the beam. Note that a concrete footing appears below the basement floor slab beneath the columns to bear and spread the weight of the imposed load.

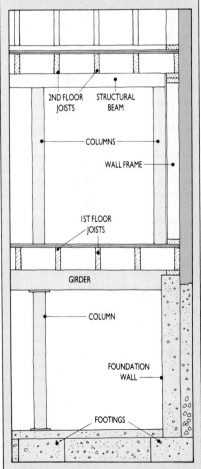

SEE ALSO

Details for:▷

House
construction   4-5
Finishing beams   15

13

SEE ALSO

◁ Details for:
Baseboards 55

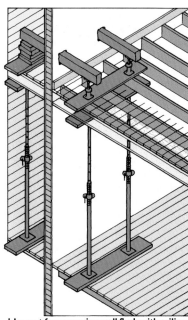

1 Layout for removing wall flush with ceiling

Supporting the wall
1 When removing a wall up to ceiling level, support the upper floor with scaffold boards and props alone when the joists pass through the brickwork to support the wall. Otherwise, in addition, use needles on jacks placed directly above the props.
2 Normally brickwork projects below the ceiling level and is supported on needles passing through holes in the wall.

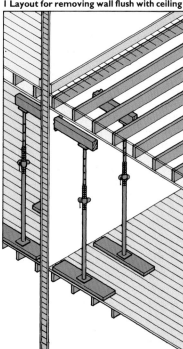

2 Layout for removing wall below ceiling

SAFE PROPPING PROCEDURE

To reduce the risk of structural collapse when opening up walls, it is critical to set up props in a safe manner. Use a level to make sure that props are exactly vertical and always use heavy boards running perpendicular to the floor joists at the bearing points of the jacks to spread the load. If the floor structure on which props are bearing seems springy, set jack posts directly beneath them on the floor below.

OPENING MASONRY WALLS

To remove part of a masonry wall you must temporarily support the wall above the opening. You will need to rent adjustable steel props and scaffold boards on which to support them. Where the beam is to be placed at ceiling level, rent extra boards to support the ceiling **(1)**. Generally you will have to fit needles through the wall to transfer the load to the props **(2)**. The needles must be at least 4 by 6 inches in section.

Rent sufficient props to be spaced not more than 3 feet apart across the width of the opening. If possible, buy the beam after the initial inspection by the building department officer's inspection. It can then be cut to your exact requirements.

Preparation and marking out
Remove the baseboards from both sides of the wall (◁). Working from one side, mark out the position of the beam on the wall in pencil. Use a steel tape measure, level and straightedge for accuracy.

Hang dust sheets around the work area on the opposite face of the wall to help contain much of the inevitable airborne dust; attach them with furring nailed over them at the top. Seal gaps around all doors with masking tape to prevent the dust from traveling throughout the house. Open windows in the rooms you're working in.

Inserting the needles
Mark the positions for the needles on the wall, then cut away the plaster locally and chisel a hole through the brickwork at each point. Finish level with the bottom of one course of bricks. Make the holes slightly oversize so you can easily pass the needles through. Position a pair of adjustable props under each needle not more than 2 feet from each side of the wall. Stand the props on scaffold boards to spread the load over the floor.

Adjust the props to take the weight of the structure and nail their base plates to the supporting boards to prevent them being dislodged.

Supporting the ceiling
If the ceiling needs supporting, stand the props on scaffold boards at each side of the wall and adjust so they're virtually to ceiling height—they should be placed 2 feet from the wall. Place another plank on top of the pairs of props and adjust simultaneously until the ceiling joists are supported.

Removing the wall
Chip off plaster with a sledgehammer and bolster chisel, then cut out the brickwork, working from the top. Once you've removed four or five courses, cut the bricks on the side of the opening. Chisel downwards, pointing towards the wall to cut the bricks cleanly. Remove all brickwork down to one course below the floorboards. Clear the rubble as you work into garbage bags—it may be worth renting a dumpster. The job is slow and laborious, but a circular saw with a masonry blade can make it easier and quicker.

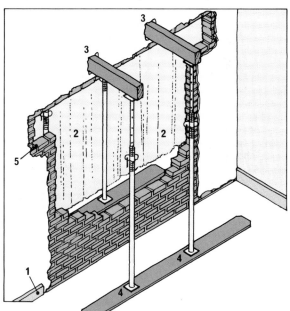

Cutting the opening
1 Remove or cut back the baseboard and mark the beam's position.
2 Hang dust sheets around the work area.
3 Cut openings and insert needles.
4 Stand props on scaffold boards and adjust them to support the needles.
5 Cut away the plaster, then chisel out the bricks starting from the top of the opening.

PLACING THE BEAM

FINISHING THE BEAM

Masonry supports for a beam

A rolled steel I-beam may be used for a lintel to support masonry above a large opening. In loadbearing cavity walls, the ends of a beam can usually be supported in notches cut into the wall itself that are fitted with a solid concrete masonry unit (CMU) to serve as the bearing surface. A structural engineer or building inspector should decide whether the wall structure and foundation can support the concentrated load transmitted by the beam ends. When the foundation structure is inadequate, or where there is no foundation at all as in a non-loadbearing hollow block partition, masonry piers and footings must be constructed. Design of masonry piers should be left to a professional.

Installing the beam

Make two wooden forms or boxes from thick plywood or utility-grade lumber and cast concrete padstones (on which to bed the beam) to the size required by the building code. Mix the concrete to the proportions 1 part cement: 2 parts sand: 4 parts aggregate. When they are set, bed the padstones in mortar at the top of each pier. When a large padstone is required, it may be better to cast it in place: set up formwork at the required height on each side and check the level between the two sides.

Build a work platform by placing doubled-up scaffold boards between steady stepladders, or rent scaffold tower sections. You'll need assistance to lift the beam into position.

Apply mortar to the padstones, then lift and set the beam in place. Pack pieces of slate between the beam and the brickwork above to fill the gap. An alternate method is to pack the gap with a mortar mix of 1 part cement: 3 parts sand, which is just wet enough to bind it together. Work it well into the gap with a bricklaying trowel and compact it with a wooden block and a hammer. Where the gap can take a whole brick or more, apply a bed of mortar and rebuild the brickwork on top of the beam. Work the course between the needles so that when they are removed the holes can be filled in to continue the bonding. Allow two days for the mortar to set, then remove the props and needles and fill in the holes.

When the beam is fitted against ceiling joists you can use a different method. Support the ceiling with props and a board to spread the load (see left), on each side of the wall. Cut away the wall, lift the beam into position and fit a pair of adjustable props under it. Apply mortar to the top of the beam and adjust the props to push it against the joists and brickwork above. Bed the padstones in mortar or build formwork at each end and cast them.

A steel beam should be enclosed to provide protection from fire (which would cause it to distort) and to give a flat surface that can be decorated. Wet plaster, gypsum wallboard or a specially made fireproof board can be used.

Cladding with plaster
Box in a beam with galvanized wire lath to provide a key for the plaster. Fold the mesh around the beam, then lap it onto the brickwork above and secure with galvanized nails.

Alternatively, wedge-shaped wooden blocks (soldiers) into the recessed sides of the beam and nail the metal lath to these. It's a good idea to prime the cut edges of the lath to prevent corrosion, which can stain the plaster.

Boxing in with wallboard
To box in the beam with wallboard, you will need to fit shaped wooden blocks, wedged into the sides. To these, fix wooden furring nailed together to make nailers for the wallboard panels. (If you plan to install a folding door system in the opening, you can nail the door jamb directly to these same nailers.) Set the wallboard about 1/8-inch below plaster level to allow for a skim coat to finish flush with the surrounding wall. Fill and seal the joints with tape compound (▷).

Plaster the piers, then finish the beam and pier together.

Disguising the beam
You can conceal a steel I-beam by fitting a simulated oak beam, molded from rigid urethane foam plastic, which can be simply glued or nailed over the beam, to give a country cottage effect to the room.

SEE ALSO
Details for:▷
Finishing wallboard 46
Fitting doors 58

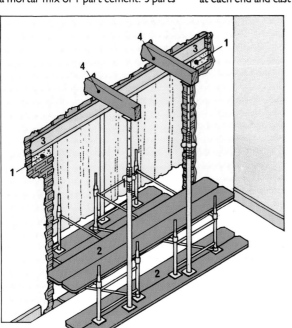

Installing the beam
1 Cast concrete padstones and set them on the brickwork piers.
2 Set up a secure platform to enable two people to work safely.
3 Place the beam on the mortared padstones and check level. Fill the gaps between the beam and the brickwork.
4 When set, remove the props and needles and fill the holes.

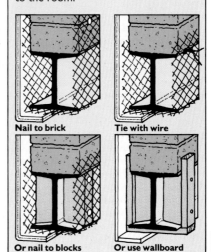

Nail to brick — Tie with wire
Or nail to blocks — Or use wallboard

15

CREATING INTERIOR ARCHES

When opening a partition wall to create one room from two or when creating a passage from one room to another, it may be desirable to create a finished opening in the form of an arch. Methods of constructing and finishing arches with gypsum wallboard and plaster are discussed below.

Wire lath-plaster arches

To create a plaster arch, first construct a frame as if you were going to finish the walls with wallboard, except you don't need to create the scored plywood arch. Apply wire lath to the framing with galvanized or blued fasteners and form the curve of the arch with a strip of wire lath. Fasten the strip to the inside of the rough jamb and to the supporting members overhead. Where the edges of the lath lining the inside of the arch meet with those of the lath on the wall surface, tie the corners together with wire. Apply plaster to the lath in two or more coats, with the first being brown coat or rough plaster followed by smooth coats (◁).

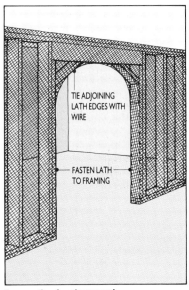

TIE ADJOINING
LATH EDGES WITH
WIRE

FASTEN LATH
TO FRAMING

Preparation for plaster arch

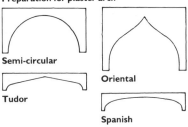

Semi-circular

Tudor

Oriental

Spanish

When designing an arch, proportion and style are key elements. A variety of arch profiles is illustrated above

Plywood-wallboard arch construction

Begin by framing a rectangular opening using 2-by-4 lumber to establish the overall height and width of the arch. Then, based on a scale drawing, determine the best locations for framing members that will run tangent to the arc and provide fastening points for a plywood strip that will be bent to form the curve. These framing members may either be lengths of 2-by-4 set at an angle between the header and rough sidejambs as shown in the drawing at the right, or vertical cripple studs cut to suitable lengths and angles to match the curve of the arch. Using the method of framing with cripples over the arch is the more difficult of the two methods.

Once the framing members are in place, rip a piece of ½-inch plywood to a width equal to that of the framing—if 2-by-4 is being used, then the correct width for the plywood would be 3½-inches. Then, set a portable circular saw to a depth of about ⅜-inch and cut saw kerfs spaced about ½-inch apart across the back of the plywood strip in the areas that must be bent to create the curve. The series of kerfs makes the plywood flexible.

Begin attaching the plywood strip at lower corner formed by the vertical rough jamb and floor. The saw kerfs should be oriented toward the framing, not facing into the opening. Drywall screws 1¼-inches long may be used as fasteners. Continue along working upward and toward the opposite side of the arch until the plywood is in place and the structural frame achieves rigidity. In some cases, it may be desirable to apply two layers of plywood to form the arch for extra stability.

Apply a strip of gypsum wallboard directly to the plywood. If the curve is relatively sharp, it may be necessary to moisten the back of the wallboard with a damp sponge to keep it from cracking as it is bent and fastened. After applying wallboard to the inside of the arch, apply it to the wall surfaces. Then apply corner beads where raw wallboard edges meet and finish with tape and wallboard compound (◁). It will be necessary to make parallel cuts along one of the flanges of the corner bead to make it flexible enough to conform to the arch. The cut flange is positioned against the vertical wall for installation, and each tab should be fastened.

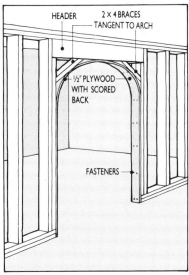

HEADER   2 X 4 BRACES
TANGENT TO ARCH

½" PLYWOOD
WITH SCORED
BACK

FASTENERS

Framing preparation for wallboard arch

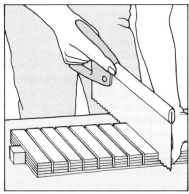

To make plywood easily bendable, cut saw kerfs across the back just deep enough to leave one of the veneer faces intact

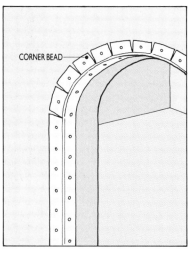

CORNER BEAD

To make corner bead flexible enough to conform to the shape of a wallboard arch, cut a series of notches in one of the flanges

REMOVING A NON-LOADBEARING WALL

Lightweight partition walls which are not loadbearing can be removed safely without consulting the authorities for approval and without the need to add temporary supports. You must, however, be certain that the wall is not structural before doing so, as some partitions do offer partial structural support.

Dismantling a stud partition

Remove the baseboards from both sides of the wall and any other moldings. It's a good idea to save these for re-use or repairs in the future. If any electrical switches or socket outlets are attached to the wall, they must be disconnected and re-routed before work begins.

Removing the plasterwork
Use a claw hammer or wrecking bar to remove the plaster and laths or wallboard cladding covering the wall frame. Once stripped to the framework, remove the vertical studs. Gather the debris which collects during stripping and remove it for disposal.

Removing the framework
First knock away any nailed bracing from between the studs. If the studs are nailed to the head and sill, they can be knocked apart. If they are difficult to remove, saw through them (at an angle to prevent the saw binding). If you make the cut close to the joint, you will be left with a useful length of re-usable lumber for future work.

Pry off the top and toe plates from the ceiling joists and floor. If the end studs are nailed to the walls, pry them away from the wall with a wrecking bar.

Finishing off
Fill the gap in the ceiling and walls, fitting a narrow strip of wallboard if necessary (▷). Fit floorboards together to close the gap if the boards are not continuous.

Dismantling a blockwork wall

Partition walls are sometimes made using lightweight concrete blocks (▷). To remove the wall, start to cut away the individual units with a bolster chisel and sledgehammer from the top. Work from the middle out to the sides.

Cut away an area of plaster first, so that you can locate the joints between blocks, then drive your chisel into these to lever them out.

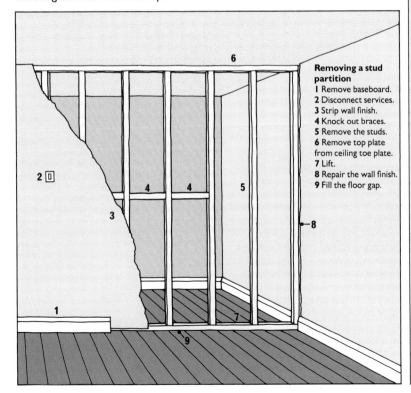

Removing a stud partition
1 Remove baseboard.
2 Disconnect services.
3 Strip wall finish.
4 Knock out braces.
5 Remove the studs.
6 Remove top plate from ceiling toe plate.
7 Lift.
8 Repair the wall finish.
9 Fill the floor gap.

METHODS OF CLOSING A FLOOR GAP

When you remove a wall to create one room from two or part of a wall to create a passage, a gap may be left in the finish flooring where the toe plate of the wall had been fastened to the subflooring.

If a gap runs parallel to the direction of the boards in wood strip flooring, you can fill it with little disturbance to the pattern. Since floor boards are generally milled with a tongue on one edge and a groove on the other so that they interlock when they are installed, fitting new boards into a confined space can present a problem. If the protuding tongue of an existing floorboard will not allow you to set the filler board in place, chisel away the lower edge of the wood that forms the groove to compensate for the obstruction. If the filler board must be ripped to a narrower width to fit into the space, cut a rabbet to fit over the tongue.

If the gap runs perpendicular to the existing flooring, it will look better to fill it with strips running in the same direction rather than with short strips to match the existing pattern. In this case, match the groove side of a filler board against the ends of existing flooring at one side of the gap and fasten with finish nails driven through the tongue. This technique is called "blind-nailing." Fit the grooves of subsequent rows over the tongues of installed strips and fasten in the same way. To fit the final strip in place, remove the tongue with a chisel or rip the board to the correct width from the tongue edge. The last strip will need to be face-nailed in place.

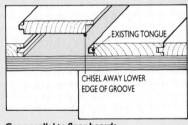

EXISTING TONGUE

CHISEL AWAY LOWER EDGE OF GROOVE

Gap parallel to floor boards

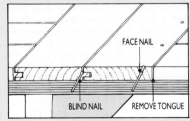

FACE NAIL

BLIND NAIL   REMOVE TONGUE

Gap perpendicular to floor boards

ALIGNING MISMATCHED FLOORS

When a partition wall separating two rooms is removed or when an opening is made to create a passageway, it is sometimes the case that the levels of the finished flooring on the two sides of the wall are at different heights. This occurs most frequently when the finished flooring of one room is different from the other, or when a floor has been refinished during a previous remodeling project.

For the sake of both appearance and safety, it is desirable either to create a uniform level or to provide an appropriate transition between the two levels. Several possible solutions to the problem are discussed below.

Treating slight mismatches

The slightest mismatches in floor levels can create tricky steps that cause people to trip, perhaps because of the unconscious habit of lifting one's feet only a certain amount while walking. When a slight mismatch exists, it is desirable to create a distinct visual transition between the two floor surfaces.

For example, a slight mismatch could exist when one part of a floor surface is finished with ceramic tile and the remainder with wood strip flooring. Ordinarily, the tile floor could be anywhere from ¼- to ⅞-inches higher than the wood floor, attributable to the thickness of the subflooring beneath the tile plus the tile thickness. Three simple treatments would be possible for addressing this problem.

The first would be to install a saddle to cover the gap left by the wall that has been removed. The best way to do this would be to fill the gap with wood blocks or strips level with the wood floor. The saddle, a stock molding available in several widths at any lumber yard, would then be nailed in place over the filler blocks. The top of the saddle should be level with or slightly higher than the higher of the two surfaces.

A second alternative here would be to nail a quarter-round molding to the tile subflooring's edge. This would provide the appropriate visual transition and also would protect the tile edge from cracking.

A third solution that would unify the room and address a slight mismatch in floor levels would be to fill the gap left where the wall was removed with a proprietary cementitious floor-filling compound finished with a slope to make the transition from one level to the other. The entire floor surface could then be covered with carpeting.

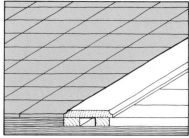

Creating a uniform floor level
Install nailing blocks in gap and nail saddle to blocks.

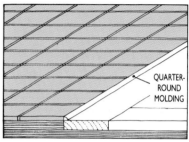

Filling gap with wood flooring strips
Install a quarter-round molding to finish and protect tile edge.

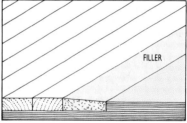

Filling gap with cementitious filler
Slope the patch from one level to the other. Finish with carpet or sheet flooring.

Building up floor levels

Where you want to create a uniform floor level in two rooms that have been made into one by removal of a partition, it may be necessary to build up the existing floor to create a flat, uniform plane. The method and materials you choose for the job should be based on the actual differential between the existing floors. Essentially, building-up methods involve compensating for the height differential between two levels with new subflooring and/or sleepers, which are strips of material installed below the subflooring where they act as spacers.

Before you make a decision on one of the specific approaches illustrated on this page, it is important to consider what type and thicknesses of materials constitute adequate subflooring for various floor finishes. Plywood, particleboard, tempered hardboard, and fiberboard are generally used for subflooring. Pine, plywood, and hardboard strips may be used for sleepers. Ceramic and resilient tile and laminated wood flooring units require a fairly rigid subfloor to prevent them from flexing underfoot, which will ultimately loosen the adhesive and may result in cracking. For these applications, minimum thicknesses of ½-inch plywood or ⅝-inch particleboard are recommended. If these materials are to be supported by sleepers, the spacing between them should be no greater than 16 inches. Tempered hardboard should be used as subflooring for tile units only if it is laid directly over an existing floor without sleepers. Solid wood strip flooring, which is generally 1 inch thick, can be nailed directly to an existing strip floor, to any existing sturdy subfloor or perpendicular to sleepers spaced 16 inches apart. Sleepers and subflooring should be fastened either with screws or ring nails that resist popping. Fasteners should be approximately three times longer than the thickness of the material being fastened. Adhesive can be used along with fasteners.

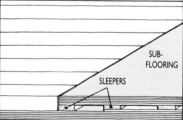

Building up lower floor surface
Match the higher surface with sleepers and subflooring. Treat subflooring or both surfaces.

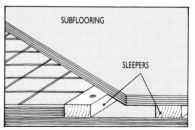

Setting sleepers
Use sleepers equal in thickness to the differential between floor levels on the lower surface and nail subflooring over both surfaces.

MAKING ONE ROOM INTO TWO

Constructing partitions to divide larger spaces into smaller ones or to alter an existing floor plan is, for the most part, a relatively simple matter of constructing one or more stud walls and finishing with gypsum wallboard or any other appropriate material. Considerations relating to codes, design goals and methods of construction are discussed on the following pages.

Code considerations

Code regulations concerning the construction of partition walls vary widely from locale to locale, but in general, they relate to the amount and type of ventilation that must be provided within an enclosed space, minimum dimensions for hallways, and fire-safety provisions. For example, most rooms that can be categorized as living space (living rooms, dining areas, bedrooms, and the like) must have windows of a certain size in relation to the square footage of the room in order to provide minimally adequate light and ventilation. Bathrooms and kitchens, while not necessarily required to have windows, often are required to have mechanical ventilation.

With respect to fire regulations, the type and thickness of materials used to construct partitions are frequently specified to ensure that walls can withstand or contain fire for a minimum of one hour. In multiple dwellings in some urban areas, metal studs are frequently required and wood studs are not permitted.

Many local codes specify that hallways may be no less than 3 feet wide to provide sufficient room for passage. While it is a good idea to consult with a professional who can advise you on local code standards relating to your particular project, it is also important to think through the space requirements for activities and room furnishings so that you will arrive at a workable, comfortable design.

Positioning a partition

The frame for a partition wall is generally made from 2-by-3 or 2-by-4 lumber and consists of a top plate, which is attached to the ceiling, a toe plate, which is attached to the floor, and studs, which run vertically between the top and toe plates (▷). While it is not usually necessary to remove the existing ceiling, floor or wall finish to fasten new wall frame components to existing structural elements in the house, it is nevertheless important to make sure fasteners used for the top and toe plates and those used to attach end studs to existing walls are driven into existing structural members. As a rule of thumb, use fasteners that are two to three times as long as the plate is thick.

Determine first whether the new partition will run perpendicular or parallel to existing floor and ceiling joists. If it will run perpendicular, then be sure to establish the exact locations of the joists (floor joists are usually spaced on 16-inch centers, ceiling joists on 16- or 24-inch centers), and drive fasteners through the plates and into the joists. If the partition is to run parallel with joists, center the plates on a joist or add blocking between existing joists to provide structural anchoring for fasteners. An end stud that is used to fasten a new partition to an existing wall should be nailed or screwed to a stud in the existing wall. Use expansion bolts to anchor to masonry walls.

Parts of a stud partition
1 Top plate
2 Toe plate
3 Wall-fastening stud
4 Stud
5 Cross-bracing

FRAMING TO REDUCE SOUND TRANSMISSION

While constructing stud walls finished with gypsum wallboard is a simple, convenient way to attain visual privacy, the conventional system of framing and finishing affords relatively low resistance to sound transmission. The typical wall, framed with 2-by-4s and finished with ½-inch wallboard, has an STC rating of only 30 to 34—STC is the standard by which resistance to sound transmission is measured.

Filling stud cavities with batt insulation and using thicker wallboard, even doubling the layers of wallboard, will improve the resistance to sound transmission. One of the most effective approaches to the problem, however, is to modify the wall framing method by using lumber for the top and toe plates that is wider than that used for the studs. Studs are then fastened in place on 8-inch centers, with edges alternately aligned with opposite edges of the plates. This reduces the amount of sound-induced vibration that is transmitted from one side of the wall to the other. The STC rating of the model illustrated below, which uses 2-by-4 studs set on 2-by-6 plates and is finished with double layers of ⅝-inch wallboard, would have an STC rating of 50 to 54—nearly equal to that of a 7-inch-thick brick cavity wall.

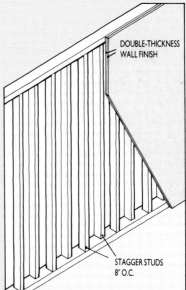

DOUBLE-THICKNESS WALL FINISH

STAGGER STUDS 8" O.C.

Wall framing and finishing design to reduce sound transmission

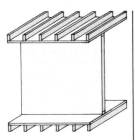

Perpendicular to joists
Drive fasteners through plates at 16- or 24-in. intervals anchoring them in joists.

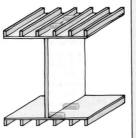

Parallel to joists
Center plates on joists and drive fasteners through them and into joists.

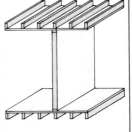

Parallel, between joists
Install perpendicular blocking between joists to serve as anchoring points for plates.

BUILDING A STUD PARTITION

Making a stud partition wall is the easiest way to divide a room in two: you can construct a plain wall, or add a doorway, pass-through or glazed area to "borrow" light from an existing window. You can build the partition directly onto the

floorboards or the joists below. The ends of the partition can be set against the existing wall finish provided there is a stud or other solid material directly beneath it, or the existing wall can be opened to add the necessary structural member.

Marking out and spacing the studs

Mark the position of one edge of the toe plate for the new wall on the floor in chalk. Use a length of 2-by-4 as a guide to draw the line. Continue the guidelines up the walls at each side, using a level and straight-edged plank or a plumb line and bob. Continue the guidelines onto the ceiling, by snapping a chalk line onto the surface with a taut string (**1**).

Spacing the studs
Lay the top and toe plates together with their face sides facing upward. Mark the position of the studs at 16-inch centers working from one edge. Square the lines across both members against a square (**2**). Center a 2-by-4 scrap over the layout marks and use the edges as a guide for marking the stud positions.

If you are fixing ⅝-inch wallboard or tongued-and-grooved (T&G) paneling, the 2-foot spacing can be used.

Marking out a doorway
If you are including a doorway in the wall, make an allowance for the width of the opening (◁). The studs that form the sides of the opening must be spaced apart by the width of the door plus a ¼-inch tolerance gap and the thickness of both door jambs. Mark the width of the opening on the top plate at the required positions, then mark the positions for the studs working from the opening. Take the dimensions for the sill from the head and cut both plates to length (**3**). The door studs overlap the ends of the sills, which must be cut back to allow for them.

Attaching the framework

Secure the toe plate to the floor on each side of the door opening using 16d common nails or 4-inch lag screws. Use the top plate as a guide to keep a toe plate interrupted by a door opening in line.
 Prop the top plate against the ceiling on its line and check that the stud marks are true with the toe plate using a plumb line. Nail or screw it to the joists (**4**).
 Measure the distance between the top and toe plate at each end and cut the outer wall studs to length: they should be a tight fit between the sill and head plate. Fasten the end studs to the walls with nails or screws.

Attaching door studs
Cut the door studs to fit between the

top plate and floor. Wedge them in place but do not fasten them yet. Add together the door height and the thickness of the finished header plus ⅜-inch for tolerance, then mark the position of the underside of the header on the edge of one stud. Hold a level on this mark and transfer it accurately to the other door stud.

Attaching the rough header
Nail the door studs to the toe plate and fasten them into the ends of the toe plates (◁). Hold the rough header in position and drive 16d nails through the studs and into the header ends. Fit cripple studs as needed between the rough header and the top plate.

Alternative fastening for door studs

An alternative method for attaching the door studs is to cut the door studs to the required door height and double-up with a stud between the top and toe plates on each side of the rough jamb. Support the door header and nail it to the top of the door studs. Cut a short length of 2-by-4 to fit vertically between the center of the top plate and header. That short stud is called a

"cripple." Secure in place by toe-nailing. Make sure when nailing all the parts together that their faces are flush and that the studs are plumb. The header must be level. The overall size of the rough opening must be large enough to accommodate the new door with necessary clearances, the finished jamb and some shim space for squaring it up.

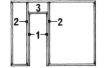

Double door studs
1 Rough jamb studs
2 Full studs
3 Rough header

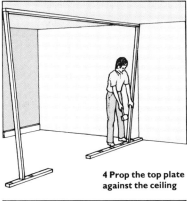

I Snap a chalk line onto the ceiling

2 Mark the top and toe plate together

3 Mark a door opening on the top plate first

4 Prop the top plate against the ceiling

5 Nail the studs to the rough header

STUD PARTITIONS

Fastening studs and braces

Measure and cut each full-length stud and fasten in turn (see below). Cut the braces to fit between the studs, and working from the wall, toe-nail the first end to the wall stud then nail through the next stud into the end of the brace. One or two rows of braces may be required: if you are going to fit wallboard horizontally, place the center of the braces at 4 feet, working from the ceiling. When the boards are to be fitted vertically, space the line of braces evenly, staggering them to make the fastening easier.

Space studs equally and nail top and bottom

Nail braces between studs to stiffen them

Fastening to an existing stud wall

Stud partitions are used for interior walls of rooms. If your new partition meets a wood-framed wall, align it with the existing solid frame members.

Fasten the wall stud of the new partition to a stud in the existing wall, where possible. Locate the stud by tapping, then drill closely spaced holes through the finish to find its center.

When the new partition wall falls between the studs of the original one, fasten its studs to the braces, top and toe plates of the original wall. Construct the new wall as above but, in this instance, cut the wall stud to fit between the floor and the ceiling and fix it before the top and toe plate are nailed into place.

Fastening wallboard vertically

Start at the doorway with the edge of the first board flush with the stud face. Before fastening, cut a 1-inch-wide strip, from the edge down to the bottom edge of the door header.

Fasten the board with 1¼- or 1½- inch wallboard nails not more than 12 inches apart. Fit the boards on both sides of the doorway then cut and fit a section over the opening. Allow a ⅛-inch gap at the cut joint. Fit the remaining boards.

Fastening wallboard horizontally

Wallboard can be fitted horizontally where it is more economical or convenient to do so. First nail the top line of boards in place so that, should it be necessary to cut the bottom run of boards, the cut edge will fall behind the baseboard. Cut a strip from the edge of the boards on each side of the doorway to allow for the sheets over the door to be fastened to the studs.

Temporarily nail a horizontal support strip to the studs ⅛-inch below the center line of the braces. Sit a board on the strip and nail it to the studs. Fit the remainder of the top boards in this way; then fit the bottom row. Stagger the vertical joints.

A second person should assist you by holding the wallboard steady. If you have to work alone, use a length of lumber to prop the board while you work. Nail from the center of the board.

NAILING TECHNIQUES

Use two 10d common nails to toe-nail each butt joint, one through each side. Temporarily nail a block behind the stud to prevent it moving sideways when driving in the first nail. Blocks cut to fit between each stud can be permanently nailed in place to form housings for extra support.

Alternative stud-nailing method

For a more rigid frame, set the studs into ½-inch-deep housings notched into the top and toe plates before nailing.

Toe-nailing
Toe-nail the butt joints with two nails.

Nailing techniques
Support the stud with a block while driving the first nail.

Supporting joint
Blocks fastened to each side brace the joint.

Housing joints
Housing joints ensure a true and rigid frame.

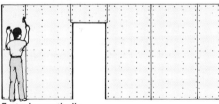

Fastening vertically
Work away from a doorway or start at one end.

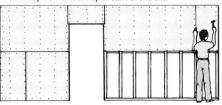

Fastening horizontally
Fix the top row first, stagger the joints on the next.

BUILDING A STAGGERED PARTITION

A stud wall can be built to divide one room into two and provide alcoves for storage at the same time. The method of construction is the same as described for the straight partition (◁) but also includes right-angle junctions. Constructing a staggered partition with a door at one end and a spacious alcove, as shown below, makes sensible use of available space.

Building the wall
1 Mark toeplate positions.
2 Transfer the marks to the ceiling.
3 Cut and fasten the toeplates to the floor.
4 Fix the top plates to the the ceiling.
5 Make corners from three studs.
6 Fasten the other studs at required spacing.
7 Fit braces, then fasten the wall finish.
8 Fit door frame and complete the wall finish.
9 Fit door jamb, door and moldings.

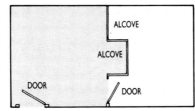

A staggered partition will form storage alcoves on each side, one for each room.

Positioning the wall

Mark out the toeplate position of the main partition across the floor. Mark the position of the "recessed" partition parallel with it. For clothes storage the recess should be at least 2 feet deep.

Calculate the length of the wall segments by setting them out on the floor. Starting from the wall adjacent to the doorway measure off the thickness of a stud, the door jamb, the width of

the door and the finished jamb. Also add ¼-inch for clearance around the door. This takes you to the face of the first short partition that runs parallel to the wall. Measure from this point to the other wall and divide the dimension in two. This gives you the line for the other short partition. Set out their thicknesses at right angles to the main partitions.

Fastening the top and toeplates

Mark the positions for the top plates on the ceiling. Use a straightedge and level or a plumb line to ensure that the marks exactly correspond with those marked on the floor.

Cut and fasten the toe and top plates to the floor and ceiling respectively, as for erecting a straight partition. Cut and fit the studs at the required spacing to suit the thickness of the wall finish.

CONSTRUCTING THE CORNERS

The right-angled corners and the end of the short partition, which supports the door frame, need extra studs to provide a nailing surface for the wallboard.

Make up a corner from three studs arranged and nailed in place. Fit short cutoffs of studs as spacer blocks. Fasten the cutoffs level with the cross-braces. Fit the boards with one edge overlapping the end of the adjoining panel. For the end of the short partition, fit two studs spaced 1½-inches apart with spacer blocks in between. Nail the board to the two faces of the partition. Leave the end exposed until the door frame is fitted.

Measure and cut the door studs, top plate and door header to length. Nail the top plate in place and fasten one stud to the room wall and one to the stud wall. Make sure they are square and flush with the end of the partition. Fit the door header and cripple stud above it. Apply wall finish over the doorway and to the side faces of the studs, including the end of the wall.

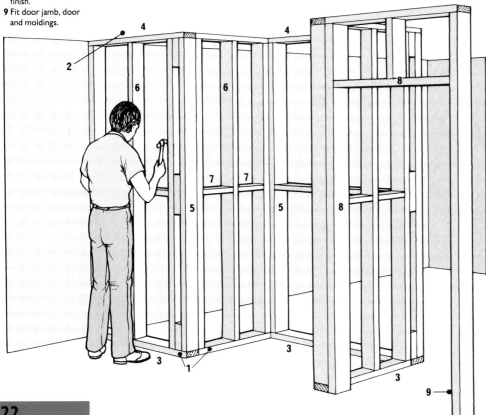

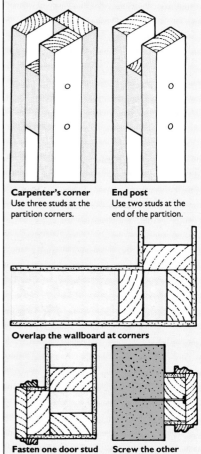

Carpenter's corner
Use three studs at the partition corners.

End post
Use two studs at the end of the partition.

Overlap the wallboard at corners

Fasten one door stud to the partition

Screw the other stud to wall

Unlike solid walls of brick or block, stud walls are mainly hollow, presenting problems when wall fixtures are to be hung. Wherever possible fixtures should be fastened directly to the structural stud members for maximum support, but if the positions of fixtures are pre-planned, extra studs, braces or mounting boards can be incorporated before the wall finish is applied.

Mounting a hand basin

A wall-mounted hand basin will need a sound enough fastening system to carry its own weight and that of someone leaning on it when it is in use.

Buy the basin before building the wall—or work from the manufacturer's literature, which usually specifies the distance between centers for fixing the brackets—and position two studs to take the mounting screws. Mark the center lines of the studs on the floor before applying the wallboard, then draw plumbed lines from the marks up the face of the sheets. Measure the height from the floor for the brackets and fasten them securely with wood screws.

Another approach would be to mount a plywood mounting board to fit between a pair of standard spaced studs

to carry both the basin and the faucets. Use exterior-grade plywood at least ¾-inch-thick. Plywood is tougher and more stable than ¾-pine and chipboard doesn't hold screws well.

Screw 2-by-2 nailing strips to the inside faces of the studs, set back from their front edges by the thickness of the board. Cut the board to size with enough height to support the basin, then screw it to the nailers to lie flush with the two studs.

Apply the wall finish to the side of the wall that will carry the basin, leaving the other side open for water-supply pipes and vent lines. Drill holes in the studs for pipes. Fasten the basin support brackets, preferably with bolts.

To hide the plumbing within the wall pass the waste pipe through a hole drilled in the wall toe plate and run it under the floor. If the waste pipe must run sideways in the wall, notch the studs (see below).

Fitting a wall cupboard

It is not always possible to arrange studs as needed for wall mounting because walls tend to be put up well before fixtures are considered. If there are no studs where you want them you will have to use hollow-wall fasteners

instead. Choose a type that will adequately support the cabinet.

Hanging shelving

Wall-mounted bookshelves have to carry a considerable weight and must be mounted securely, especially to stud partitions. Use shelving that has strong metal uprights into which adjustable brackets may be locked. Screw into studs if you can; otherwise use suitable hollow-wall fasteners (see below right).

Hanging small fixtures

Load-carrying fixtures with a small contact area can crush the wall finish and strain the fasteners. Mount coat hooks on a board to spread the load, and screw the boards to studs. Hang small pictures on picture hooks secured with steel pins, large ones on a double-pin type, preferably fastened to a stud. Put mirror plates on the frame of a heavy mirror or picture for screw mounting. Use stranded wire for mirrors hung on a hook fastened to a stud.

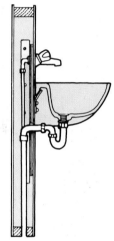

Mounting a basin ▶
Fasten a wall-mounted basin to an exterior-grade plywood board.

FITTING PIPES AND WIRES IN STUD PARTITIONS

It is easy to plan and fit pipes and wires in a stud partition wall before finishing it. To guard against future occupants drilling into them, set horizontal cables or pipes no more than 12 inches above floor level.

Plumbing
Plan the runs of supply or waste pipes by marking the faces of the vertical studs or the cross-braces. Remember that a waste pipe must have a slight fall. When you are satisfied with the layout, cut notches in the studs for the pipes (see right).

Transfer the marked lines to the sides of the studs or braces and drill holes for the pipes close to their front edges. Cut into the holes to make notches. If cut at a slight angle they will hold the pipes while they are being fitted.

Notches cut for waste pipes must be reinforced to prevent them from weakening the studs. Drill the holes in the centers of the studs, following the

pipe run. Before cutting into the holes, cut housings for 1-by-2 furring strips to bridge the notches. Make the notches, set the waste pipe in place, then screw the bridging pieces into their housings flush with the fronts of the studs.

Cross-braces need not be reinforced, but fit one under a pipe bend as a support.

Running electric cable
Drill ½-to ¾-inch holes at the centers of the studs for level runs of cable, and in cross-braces for vertical runs. When possible, it is most convenient to mount electrical boxes for switches and outlets directly to studs. Boxes are available with a number of different types of brackets for this purpose. Boxes with gripping arms are also available for mounting boxes directly to cutouts in wallboard. Surface-mounted boxes may also be used.

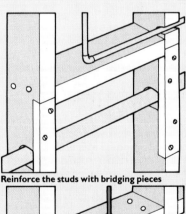

Reinforce the studs with bridging pieces

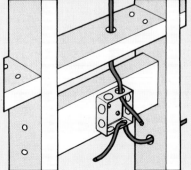

Fit metal boxes to a mounting board

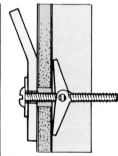

Toggle bolt

Hollow wall fasteners
Various fasteners may be used for insertion into holes and securing with screws or bolts. Some expand to grip the lining as a screw is tightened; some are held in place by a toggle that springs out behind the wall finish.

METAL STUD PARTITIONS

Metal stud and track systems are increasingly being used for wall and ceiling framing in residential construction. Somewhat more economical than wood, metal wall framing components can prove, with a little experience, to be faster and easier to work with than conventional framing. What follows is a discussion of the basic system components, the tools necessary for working with them and some basic approaches to interior, nonstructural framing tasks.

Metal framing components

The basic parts of metal framing systems are studs, which are C-shaped in section view, and track, which is U-shaped. Metal studs have holes punched along their broad surface to permit the passage of wiring or piping and also to serve as mounts for metal cross-bracing, which may be used to stiffen wall frames. Metal track, which is essentially used for top, toe and ledger plates, does not have holes.

Stud and track are available in widths that correspond to the actual dimensions of ordinary framing lumber:

2-by-2s, 2-by-3s, 2-by-4s and 2-by-6s. Available lengths for studs also correspond to those of dimension lumber, starting at 8 feet and increasing in increments of 2 feet up to 20 feet. Track generally comes in 10-foot lengths.

In addition to stud and track, of interest to do-it-yourselfers is metal furring strip. It may be used for ordinary furring-out applications such as preparing a masonry wall for a panel finish and is also sometimes used as support for suspended ceilings.

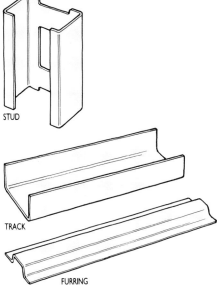

Metal framing components

Specialized tools and fasteners

Metal framing components can be cut with ordinary sheetmetal shears—aviation snips, which have a spring-action are most convenient for extensive work.

The majority of joints formed between metal framing components are fastened by crimping. A special crimping tool used for metal framing punches through the flanges of the pieces being joined and bends back the metal to create a sort of negative staple. Where greater strength is needed, joints can be fastened with ¼-inch panhead tapping screws, known as "metal-to-metal screws" in trade jargon.

Gypsum wallboard is fastened to the metal framework with "drywall screws," which are essentially Phillips-type tapping screws with a bugle head. Drywall screws are available in lengths from 1 to 3 inches and may also be used for fastening wood to metal frames. Phillips-type tapping screws with "trim heads," similar to those of finishing nails, are useful for applying wood moldings and door jambs.

It is essential to have a screwgun when working with metal studs. Similar in appearance to electric drills, screw guns have high-speed motors and magnetized chucks that hold Phillips tips needed for driving the various screws. Screwguns are also equipped with clutches and depth-finders. Once a screw is fitted to the tip and the machine is switched on, you press the

screw point against the work to engage the clutch, causing the tip to rotate. The depth-finder, once coming in contact with work surface, relieves pressure on the clutch and stops the tip from spinning once the screw has been driven to the desired depth. No. 1 Phillips tips are used to drive pan- and trim-head screws; No. 2 tips are used to drive drywall screws.

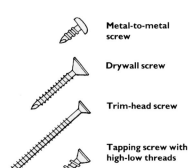

Metal-to-metal screw

Drywall screw

Trim-head screw

Tapping screw with high-low threads

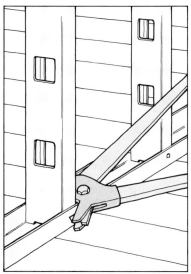

Metal stud crimper

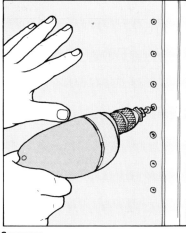

Screwgun

METAL STUD PARTITIONS

Assembling metal wall frames

After snapping layout lines on the ceiling and floor, fasten lengths of track in place to serve as top and toe plates. Use 1½-inch panhead tapping screws no greater than 24 inches apart to fasten the track to wood flooring or to ceilings where wood structural members are beneath the finish. To fasten track or furring to masonry, use either plastic anchors set in predrilled holes and panhead screws, or panhead screws with high-low threads, which will hold in masonry without plugs. Butt tracks at right angles to form corners; do not miter cut.

Cut studs to about ¼-inch shorter than the measurement from floor to ceiling and slip the studs into the tracks, spacing them 16 inches on-center. Crimp the studs in place. Studs and headers forming rough door openings should be screwed together with metal-to-metal screws. Where heavy, solid doors will be used, it is advisable to reinforce door openings with wood framing, which can easily be slipped into and fastened to the track.

A unique feature of metal stud systems is that the flanges of the track may be snipped and bent to create tabs that may be fastened to intersecting or adjacent members. V-shaped cutouts may be made in a track flange and then the broad surface of the track snipped to facilitate forming curved top and toe plates. Customized, two-sided tracks and box beams may also be created by screwing various members together lengthwise.

Apply ½- or ⅝-wallboard to the wall frame with 1¼-inch drywall screws spaced approximately 16 inches apart. Screw heads should be driven slightly below the wallboard surface, but take care not to tear the wallboard's paper binder.

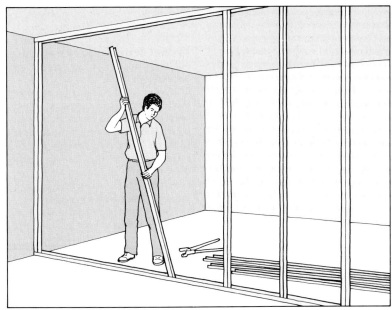

Metal studs are fitted into track that serves as top and toe plates

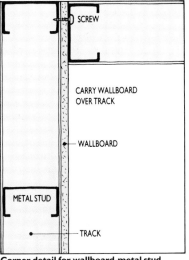

Corner detail for wallboard-metal stud assembly

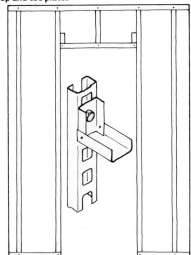

Door header assembly detail

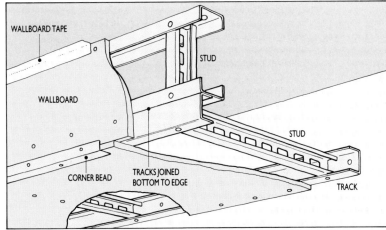

Soffit construction with metal studs and track

Box beam formed with two studs

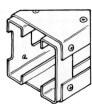

Box beam formed with two studs and pieces of track

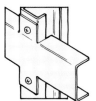

Cross-bracing for stud made by cutting track flanges and bending into tabs

Track notched to form curved plate

25

CEILINGS: LOWERING A CEILING

When the ceiling of a room presents a problem, either because of the condition of its finish or because its height makes the room seem cavernous, remodeling by lowering the ceiling may be the simplest solution. Several approaches to remodeling a ceiling are discussed on this and the following pages.

High ceilings are generally found in older houses. Some are decorative molded ceilings, while many others have simple but attractive cornice moldings, and these should be preserved to maintain the character of the house. But where a room is plain and the ceiling needs attention, or where the proportions of the room would benefit from alteration, a lowered ceiling can be an improvement. It can be used to hide ducting, improve sound and heat insulation and provide a space for flush or concealed lights.

Changing the character of a room

A room's character is largely determined by the relation of its area to its ceiling height. Low ceilings are considered charming and cozy, while tall rooms are felt to be very imposing, though they are usually larger. Other high-ceilinged rooms feel somewhat uncomfortable.

The sense of coziness or emptiness may be based on practical experience. For example, the volume of a low-ceilinged room is less than that of a high-ceilinged room of the same floor area, so it would be easier to heat evenly, and a room with an even temperature feels more comfortable than one where the temperature varies due to rising air currents. The acoustics in a small room may also be better, inducing a relaxed feeling. Yet the qualities of light and space in a room may be due to its high ceiling, and if it were lowered, changing the room's proportions, the tall windows might look awkward and the sense of space be lost.

Making a model

Making a simple cardboard model of a room's interior is a good way to check that a planned project will suit the room before spending time and money on the real thing.

Measure the length, width and height of the room and the height, width and positions of the windows and doors. Mark out and cut pieces of cardboard for the floor and walls to any convenient scale—perhaps simplest is to allow 1 inch to equal 1 foot.

Mark the positions of the doors and windows on the cardboard walls and cut out the openings with a craft knife. The openings will allow light into the finished model. You can hinge the doors in place with self-adhesive tape. Draw lines on the walls to represent the baseboards and casings around the doors and windows. You can color these details to make them more realistic. Also mark in the fireplace to the same scale. A projecting chimney breast can be formed in cardboard and glued on.

Punch a small peep-hole in each wall at a height scaled to your eye level and assemble the floor and walls using adhesive tape.

Cut a cardboard panel representing the ceiling to fit closely between the walls. If the real ceiling is to be the suspended type, with lighting around its edges, cut the panel smaller to provide the gap at the sides.

Cut two strips of cardboard about 2 inches wide and as long as the width of the ceiling piece and glue them on edge across the back of the ceiling. Cut two more strips, the same width but a little longer, and use clips to attach them to the shorter ones. The longer strips will rest across the walls and the clips are adjusted to set the ceiling at various heights. Check the effect of this on the room by viewing the interior space through the peepholes and the door and window openings.

To simulate a grid-system illuminated ceiling make a framework with strips of balsa wood to the same scale as the room and covered with tracing paper.

RECOMMENDED DIMENSIONS

The height of a new ceiling should be no less than 7 feet 6 inches. In some cases 6 feet 6 inches is acceptable under beams or bay windows.

You can construct a slightly lower ceiling in a kitchen, provided at least half of it is at 7 feet 6 inches.

In a roof space the ceiling height should be a minimum of 7 feet 6 inches for at least half the area of the room. However, this area might not represent the whole floor. Mark all the sloping ceilings to the desirable minimum height above the floor, then use a plumb line to mark the floor directly below. The area of the floor within the marked lines represents the actual area used to calculate the ceiling height.

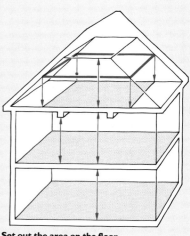

Set out the area on the floor

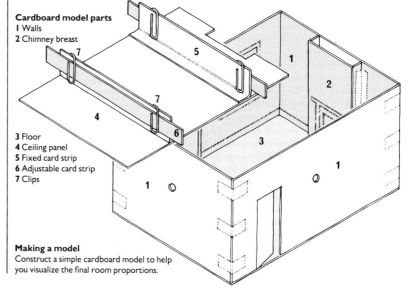

Cardboard model parts
1 Walls
2 Chimney breast
3 Floor
4 Ceiling panel
5 Fixed card strip
6 Adjustable card strip
7 Clips

Making a model
Construct a simple cardboard model to help you visualize the final room proportions.

LOWERING A CEILING: OPTIONS

You might decide to lower a ceiling for practical reasons or simply to change the style of the interior, but whatever the reason, you should consider your options carefully because a ceiling is a large area which can be costly to cover.

Wood framed ceilings are heavy but they can be custom-made to suit the style and shape of a room using basic woodworking skills.

Manufactured suspended-ceiling systems are relatively lightweight, easy to install and offer a wide choice of materials for the paneling, but a strong grid pattern is unavoidable.

Use the chart to help you consider the project in advance and to compare one system with another.

PROJECT CONSIDERATIONS

Advantages of a lowered ceiling
- Improves room proportions.
- Adds decorative flair.
- Conceals poor lighting.
- Offers various lighting options.
- Conceals ducting.
- Reduces heating bills.
- Saves on decorating material costs.

Disadvantages of a lowered ceiling
- Spoils proportions of a room.
- Covers decorative features.
- Large area can be costly.
- Systems will require periodic cleaning.
- Some materials can be a fire hazard.

Points to check
- Recommended dimensions
- Consult local codes for kitchens
- Style of proposed ceiling/interior
- Ease of making
- Cost of materials
- Alternative systems

Mechanical details
- New light fittings required. Surface, recessed and concealed types are options.
- Lighting circuit will need extending.
- Provide ventilation ducts, wiring and plumbing lines.

OPTIONS (See right) ▶

LOWERED CEILING

Design features	Planning the scheme	Type of construction	Covering/finishes
Will change the room proportions. Will hide old ceiling or mechanicals. Least likely to appear a conversion. Can be fitted with cornice moldings. Without a hatch, prevents access to the void above.	Make initial sketches of the proposed interior, then draw scale plans on graph paper to detail and cost the scheme. Make a scale model to visualize the effect of the ceiling.	This type of construction uses new ceiling joists to span room in shortest direction. The joists are supported by headers fastened to the walls. Ties and hangers may be used.	Materials: Gypsum wallboard. Fire-resistant compositions. Plywood. Tongue-and-groove paneling. Mineral-fiber tiles. Finishes: papered, painted, varnished or ready-finished.

PART-LOWERED CEILING

Design features	Planning the scheme	Type of construction	Covering/finishes
Similar to the full lowered ceiling above but has added interest of the split-level. The end transition between levels can be vertical or sloped, sloped being preferable when parallel with a window.	As for lowered ceiling (see above). Consider the line of the "drop" in relation to the window. It should not cut across the window when viewed from the opposite side of the room.	Wood-frame constructions as for lowered ceiling (see above). The end framework is formed from ties and hangers. The hangers are set at an angle for a sloped end.	As for lowered ceiling (see above).

OPEN-BOARD CEILING

Design features	Planning the scheme	Type of construction	Covering/finishes
Not a true ceiling but a framework which appears to be continuous. Most effective in hallways or passage. It does not seal off the old ceiling. Can be dismantled for access to services.	As for lowered ceiling (see above). The spacing and depth of the slats can be varied: you should not be able to see between the slats when looking straight ahead.	Edge-on plank construction using no sub-structure. Perimeter planks are housed and fastened to the wall; the slats are fastened to them.	No covering is used. The ceiling and walls above the slats are painted a dark color. Finish for woodwork: light-colored stain, clear varnish or paint.

SUSPENDED CEILING

Design features	Planning the scheme	Type of construction	Covering/finishes
Appears to be suspended away from the walls and appears to float: concealed lighting enhances this illusion. Has modern character. Will mask old ceiling or mechanicals. Not demountable.	As for lowered ceiling (see above). Locate original ceiling joists and set out their position on your plan drawing: design the structure around them.	Wood-frame construction using ties fastened across ceiling joists and carrying hangers from which the new frame is suspended. The main components are assembled with bolts.	As for lowered ceiling (see above).

SUSPENDED CEILING SYSTEMS

Design features	Planning the scheme	Type of construction	Covering/finishes
A grid system manufactured from lightweight materials for self-assembly. Individual translucent or opaque panels sit in the grid framework. The system is demountable.	As for lowered ceiling (see above). Draw a plan of the room on graph paper and set out a symmetrical grid.	Lightweight alumium T-sectioned extrusions suspended from angle sections screwed to the walls. Tees are loose-fitted.	Metal: anodized. Panel materials: plain, textured and colored translucent plastic; opaque plastic; mineral fiber.

SEE ALSO

Details for:▷

Making a hatch	31
Finishing wallboard	46-47
Gypsum-board ceilings	48

Vapor checks
Provide a vapor check to prevent condensation problems in an unventilated space above a lowered ceiling. Use a waterproof wallboard, an impervious sealer or polyethylene plastic sheeting. The gaps between the boards or the plastic must be sealed effectively.

Wallboard
Bed joints in mastic.

Polyethylene sheeting
Fold and staple edges.

CONSTRUCTING A LOWERED CEILING

You can build the new ceiling at any height provided it complies with the regulations. However, the height of window openings may limit your choice. About 8 feet is a useful height for a lowered ceiling. It is a common room height for modern houses and relates to standard wallboard sheet sizes. Most manufacturers of built-in furniture adopt it as a standard height for ceilings.

Planning the layout

Making a lowered ceiling requires a considerable amount of lumber for the framework and wallboard to cover it. It is critical to select the correct width for the joists and their spacing based on their span and the weight of the ceiling finish material. Arrange the panels with the paper-covered edges set at right angles to the timber supports. Stagger the end joints between each row of boards and arrange them so as to fall on a joist.

If you plan to use tongue-and-groove paneling, buy it in lengths that can be economically cut to suit your joist arrangement, since excessive cut-offs are wasteful. Avoid butt joints coinciding on adjacent boards.

Materials for the framework

Make a cutting list of the materials you will need to make up the structure. In most cases 2-by-3 or 2-by-4 lumber can be used for the ceiling joists. These should span the room in the shortest direction. Calculate the number of joists you will need. These should be spaced at 16 or 24 inches on center according to the thickness of the wallboard (◁). These dimensions will also suit other types of paneling.

You will need extra joist lumber for the braces fitted between the joists. One-by-two strips may be fastened to walls and used as ledgers to support the ceiling frame.

Spans of over 8 feet should be supported by hangers and ties, made from lumber not less than 2-by-2 which are fastened to the ceiling above. Place the hangers about the middle of the joists' span.

It is possible to use more hangers and reduce the section of the joists from 2-by-3 to 2-by-2. In this case place the hangers about 3 feet apart.

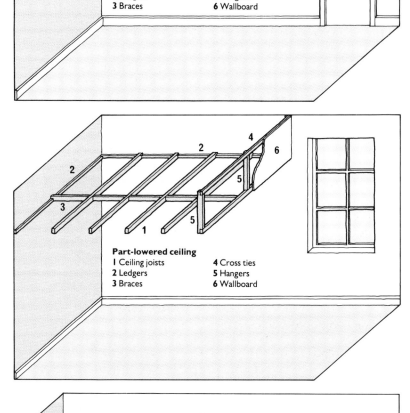

Framed lowered ceiling
1 Ceiling joists   4 Ties
2 Ledgers   5 Hangers
3 Braces   6 Wallboard

Part-lowered ceiling
1 Ceiling joists   4 Cross ties
2 Ledgers   5 Hangers
3 Braces   6 Wallboard

Open-board ceiling
1 Ledger
2 Slats
3 Dark-painted area

SUSPENDED CEILINGS WITH PERIMETER LIGHTING

Constructing the ceiling

Mark the height of the new ceiling, including the thickness of the finish on one wall. At this level draw a horizontal line across the wall using a straightedge and level for accuracy. Continue the line around the room at this height. Cut ledger boards to length. Nail or screw them to the walls at 16-inch intervals with the bottom edge level with the line.

Cut the ceiling joists to length. Notch the ends to sit over the wall ledgers to bring the bottom edges flush. Toenail the joists to the wall ledgers. Cut and fit hangers and ties to prevent long joists from sagging (see left). These supports also stiffen the structure.

Cut and nail braces between the joists to support the edges of the wallboard. Nail tapered-edged wallboard to the joists, braces and wall battening. Fill and tape the joints between boards and walls (▷).

Lowering part of a ceiling

You can lower part of a ceiling to overcome problems around tall window openings or to create a split-level effect. Follow the method for constructing a ceiling (as described above) but enclose the end-drop with wallboard nailed to hangers fixed in a line to a cross-tie member set above the last joist.

Making an open-board ceiling

One-by-six pine boards set on edge and spaced apart can be used to create a simple yet effective open-board ceiling. Smaller sections can be used where the span is short, as with a narrow hallway.

Cut four lengths of ledger strips to line the walls all around. Before nailing or screwing them at the required height, mark and cut housings in two of the planks opposite one another. Space the housings about 9 inches apart. For boards less than 6 inches wide, space them about 4 to 6 inches apart. Cut notches in the ends of the "slat" boards to sit in the housings so that the bottom edges finish flush.

Before fitting the slats, paint walls and ceilings above the lining boards with a dark flat latex paint. Also paint ducts or plumbing to disguise it. Finish the slats with varnish, stain or paint.

A suspended ceiling with reveals around the perimeter appears to float away from the walls. Fluorescent lights can be placed around the edge of the ceiling to enhance the floating effect and provide wall-washing illumination. The fiber can be covered with plasterboard, decorative veneered ply or mineral-fiber ceiling ties.

Locate the position of the ceiling joists by noting the direction of the floorboards of the room above; the joists will run at right angles to them. Pinpoint the joists from below by boring pilot holes through the ceiling. Mark the center of each joist.

Setting out the grid

Measure the lengths of the walls and draw a scaled plan of the room on graph paper. Set out the shape of the ceiling panel on the drawing with its edges approximately 8 inches from each wall. Then set out the position of the 2-by-2 ceiling ties. The ties should run at right angles to the joists of the ceiling above. The ends of the ties and sides of the two outer ones should be about 1 foot from the walls. The number of ties you'll need will depend on the size of the ceiling, but three should be a minimum. They should be spaced not more than 3 feet apart for adequate support.

Constructing the ceiling

Counterbore and securely screw the ties in position to each of the joists they cross. Cut 2-by-2 hangers to the required length and fasten them to the

ties with carriage bolts not more than 3 feet apart.

Cut additional ties to the same length as the planned ceiling panel. Bolt them across the ends of the hangers with an equal space at each end.

Cut the required number of 2-by-2 furring strips to suit the spacings necessary to support the wallboard or tiles used as a ceiling finish. The length of the furring strips should be equal to the width of the ceiling panel minus two 1-by-2 inch capping strips. Equally space and screw the furring strips to the tie members. Countersink the screw heads.

Mark off the positions of the furring strips along the sides of each capping strip. Drive 3-inch nails into, but not quite through, the cappings at these points. Apply woodworking adhesive and nail the cappings to the ends of the furring strips.

Finishing the assembly

Run electrical wiring in preparation for the fluorescent lights to be fitted. Cover the underside of the frame with wallboard, decorative veneered panels or ceiling tiles. Fill and finish the surface and edges of a gypsum wallboard ceiling. Finish the exposed edges of the frame to match other materials as required.

Wire up and fit slim fluorescent light fixtures to loose boards, which sit on top of the projecting frame. The fixtures can then be easily removed for servicing. Leave enough spare cable to allow the lights to be lifted clear.

SEE ALSO

Details for: ▷
Finishing
wallboard   46-47

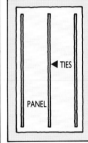

Setting out
Set out the panel on graph paper with an 8-in. gap all round. Insert the ties about 1 ft.

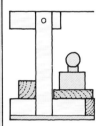

Light fixture
Attach a fluorescent light to a removable board for servicing.

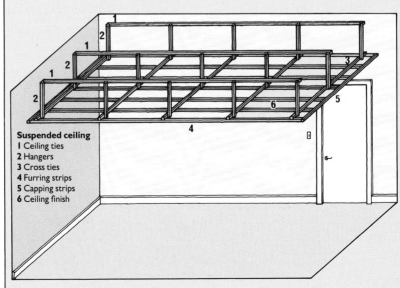

Suspended ceiling
1 Ceiling ties
2 Hangers
3 Cross ties
4 Furring strips
5 Capping strips
6 Ceiling finish

SUSPENDED CEILING SYSTEMS

Manufactured suspended-ceilings are made from slim metal sections, which provide a fairly lightweight structure for acoustic or translucent panels. They're quick and easy to fit using no special tools.

Panel layouts

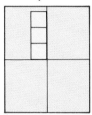

1 Main tee on center

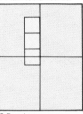

2 Panel on center

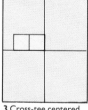

3 Cross-tee centered

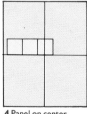

4 Panel on center

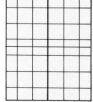

5 Best grid arrangement

The lightweight alloy framework is made from three basic elements: wall angles, which are fastened to walls; main tees, which are similar in function to joists and are usually installed across a room's shorter span; and cross-tees, which are set between and perpendicular to main tees.

The loose panels sit on the flanges of the tees. They can be easily lifted out for access to ducts or to service light fixtures, which can be concealed behind them. You need at least 4 inches of space above the framework to fit the panels.

Manufactured systems
Manufacturers offer a choice of colored framing as well as colored-translucent and opaque panels.

Setting out the grid

Normally, 2-by-2 or 2-by-4 panels are used for suspended ceiling systems. Before installing the framework, draw a plan of the ceiling on graph paper to ensure that the borders are symmetrical. Draw a plan of the room with two lines taken from the hallway point on each wall to bisect at the center. Lay out the grid on your plan.

with a main tee centered on the short bisecting line (**1**), then lay it out again with a line of panels centered on the same line (**2**). Use the grid that provides the widest border panels.

Plot the position of the cross tees in the same way, using the other line (**3, 4**). Try to get the border panels even on opposite sides of the room (**5**).

Fitting the framework

Before installing a suspended ceiling with translucent panels, remove any flaking materials and repair any cracks in the plaster ceiling above. Paint the ceiling with white latex to improve reflectivity if concealed fluorescent lighting is to be used.

Install fluorescent light fixtures as needed across the ceiling: 16 watts per square yard is recommended for a suitable level of light in most rooms.

Mark the height of the suspended ceiling on the walls with a continuous leveled line. Hacksaw two lengths of wall-angle section to fit the longest walls. Remove burrs from the ends with a file. Drill screw holes at 2-foot intervals. Drill and plug the walls using the angle as a guide and screw the components in place (**1**).

Next cut lengths of wall angle to fit the shorter walls. Their ends should fit on the angles already fitted. Attach them in the same way as the other wall-angle sections.

Mark the positions of the tees along two adjacent walls, as set out on the graph paper. Cut the main tees to span

the room. Sit them on the wall angles (**2**). Use a ceiling panel to check that they are parallel and at right angles to the wall and each other.

Cut the border of cross-tees to fit between the end of the main tees and wall angles. Set them in line with the points marked on the wall. Position the remainder of the cross-tees following the same line.

Working from the center drop in the full-sized panels. Measure and cut the border panels to fit the grid and then drop them into place.

Spanning wide rooms
If the size of the room exceeds the maximum length of the main tee, join two or more pieces together. A joint bridging piece is provided if the ends of the tees are not made to lock together.

For spans exceeding 10 feet, support the main tees with wire hangers. Fasten each wire, spaced not more than 5 feet apart, through a hole in the tee and hang it from a screw eye in a furring strip or joist in the ceiling.

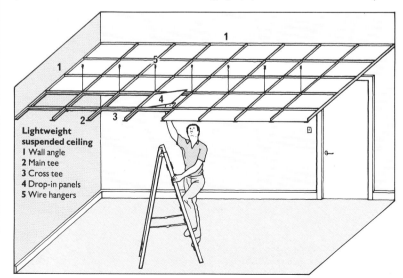

Lightweight suspended ceiling
1 Wall angle
2 Main tee
3 Cross tee
4 Drop-in panels
5 Wire hangers

1 Screw the angle to the wall

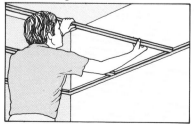

2 Position the main tees

INSTALLING A FOLDING LADDER

Access to the attic space is more convenient and safer if you install a folding ladder. Some are complete with built-in hatch cover, frame and fittings ready to install in a new opening. Normally, the length of the ladders suits standard ceiling heights, 7 feet 6 inches and 8 feet. Some can extend up to 10 feet.

Concertina ladder

To fit a concertina ladder, securely screw the brackets of the aluminum ladder to the framework of the opening. Fit the retaining hooks to the framework to support the ladder in the stowed position. Operate the ladder with a pole, which hooks over the bottom rail. Fit the hatch door to the frame with a continuous hinge, followed by a push-to-release latch installed at the edge of the hatch door.

Ready-to-install folding ladder

Cut the opening and trim the joists to the size specified by the manufacturer. Insert the casing with built-in frame in the opening and screw it to the joists.

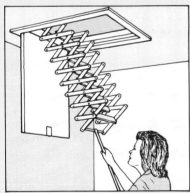

A concertina ladder is simple to install

Folding ladders are easy to deploy

MAKING AN ATTIC-ACCESS HATCH

Many houses are provided with a hatch in the ceiling to give access to the attic space for convenient storage and maintaining the roof structure. If your house has a large attic space without access from the house,

installing a hatch could be a valuable addition. Pre-fab units are available at many home centers. Although the job is basically straightforward, it does entail cutting into the top-floor ceiling structure.

When cutting into the structure of a ceiling to create an attic entrance, it is important to consider the effect of the alteration on the ability of the framing to support the existing structure. Some roof frames may incorporate purlins, these bearing part of the load on rafters. The purlins may be supported by vertical members that transfer part of the load to ceiling joists. If you have any doubts about the effect of cutting joists to install a hatchway, consult a knowledgeable professional.

If you have a choice, site the hatchway over a landing, but not close to a stair, rather than in a room. In this way a ladder used for access will not interfere with the occupants or function of the room. Allow for the pitch of the roof, as you will need headroom above the hatch.

Making the opening

If you are planning to install a special folding ladder, the size of the new opening will be specified by the manufacturer. Generally aim to cut away no more than one of the ceiling joists: these are usually spaced 16 inches apart.

Locate three of the joists by drilling

pilot holes in the ceiling. Mark out a square for the opening between the two outer joists. Cut an inspection hole inside the marked area to check that no obstacles are in the way of the cutting line. Saw through the ceiling finish and strip it away.

Pass a light into the roof space and climb up into it between the joists. Lay a board across the joists to support yourself. Saw through the middle joist, cutting it back 2 inches from each edge of the opening. Cut two new lengths of joist lumber—called headers—to fit between the joists. Nail the joints between the joists and headers. Use two 16d common nails to secure each joist.

Nail the ceiling laths or plasterboard to the underside of the header joists. Cut jambs from nominal 1-inch boards to cover the joists and the edges of the ceiling finish. Repair the damaged edges of the existing finish with filler. When the filler has set, nail a casing around the opening. Make a drop-in or hinged panel of ¾-inch plywood or particleboard. If you plan to use the attic space mainly for storage, fix chipboard panels over the joists. Cut them to fit through the opening.

SEE ALSO

Details for: ▷
House construction 4-5

Alternative ways to install hatch covers

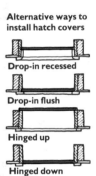

Drop-in recessed

Drop-in flush

Hinged up

Hinged down

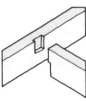

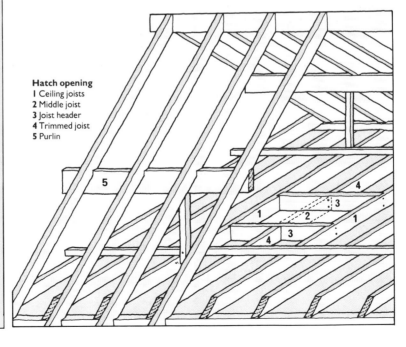

Hatch opening
1 Ceiling joists
2 Middle joist
3 Joist header
4 Trimmed joist
5 Purlin

INTERIOR WALL FINISH

Storing plaster
Keep an open bag of plaster in a plastic sack sealed with adhesive tape.

As popular interest in authentic restoration of older houses grows, there is a renewed appreciation for the qualities of a plaster wall finish. While wallboard is generally faster and easier to apply, plaster walls have a look and feel that is unmistakable to the discerning eye, and sound insulation properties that are superior to wallboard. In the following pages you will find both traditional and modern approaches to plastering as well as methods for applying and finishing wallboard.

Traditional plastering techniques

Traditional plastering uses a mix of plastering materials and water, which is spread over the rough background in one, two or three layers. Each layer is applied with a trowel and leveled accordingly; when set, the plaster forms an integral part of the wall or ceiling. Traditionally, plaster has been applied over masonry walls or wood lath, thin wood strips slightly spaced that make it possible for plaster to key-in and

adhere. More recently, metal and gypsum laths have been developed. Plastering well requires practice to achieve a smooth, flat surface over a large area. With care, an amateur can produce satisfactory results, provided the right tools and plaster are employed and the work is divided into manageable sections. All-purpose one-coat plasters are now available to make plastering easier for amateurs.

Gypsum wallboard

Manufactured boards of paper-bound gypsum are widely used to finish the walls and ceilings in modern homes and during renovations. Its use overcomes the drying-out period required for wet plasters and requires less skill to apply.

The large flat boards are nailed or bonded to walls and ceilings to provide a separate finishing layer. The surface may be decorated directly once the boards are sealed, or covered with a thin coat of finish plaster.

BUYING AND STORING PLASTER

Plaster powder is normally sold in 50- and 100-pound paper sacks. Smaller sizes, including 5-pound sacks, are available from DIY stores for repair work. It's generally more economical to buy the larger sacks, but this depends on the scale of the work. Try to buy only as much plaster as you need. It's better to overestimate, however, to allow for waste and prevent running short (◁).

Store plaster in dry conditions: if it is to be kept in an outbuilding for some time, cover it with plastic sheeting to protect it from moisture. Keep the paper bags off a concrete floor by placing them on boards or plastic sheeting. Open bags are more likely to absorb moisture, which can shorten the setting time and weaken the plaster. Keep an opened bag in a sealed plastic sack. Use self-adhesive tape to seal it. Discard plaster which contains lumps.

Ready-to-use joint compound, which can be used for some plaster repairs, is also available in plastic tubs. It can be more expensive to buy it this way but it is easier for amateurs to use and it will keep for a long time, provided the airtight lid is well sealed.

Traditional plastering
(Right)
The construction of a lath-and-plaster ceiling and plastered masonry wall.
1 Brick ground
2 Ceiling joists
3 Lath
4 Base coat
5 Brown coat
6 Finishing coat
7 Cornice molding

Drywall
(Far right)
The construction of a modern wallboard wall and ceiling.
1 Block wall
2 Furring
3 Ceiling joists
4 Cross-braces
5 Gypsum wallboard
7 Crown molding
8 Joint compound

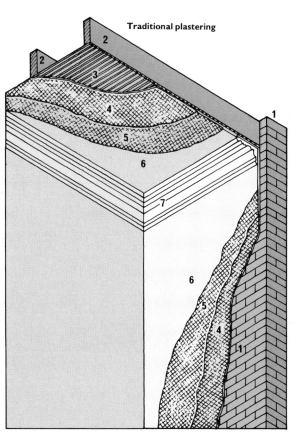

Traditional plastering

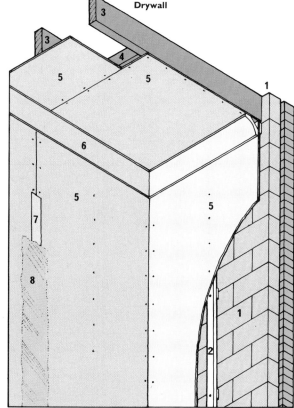

Drywall

TYPES OF PLASTER

Plastering is carried out using modern gypsum plasters or mixes based on cement, lime and sand. By varying the process and introducing additives, a range of plasters can be produced within a given type to suit different grounds, or substrate materials.

Plasters are basically produced in two grades—one as a base or floating coat, the other for finishing coats. Base coat gypsum plasters are pre-mixed types, which contain lightweight aggregates. Base-coat sanded plasters, which are based on cement or cement/lime, have to be mixed on site with a suitable grade of clean, sharp sand (although finish plasters are ready to use with the addition of water).

The following information deals only with those materials suitable for domestic work.

PLASTER TYPES AND RELATED MATERIALS

GYPSUM PLASTERS

Most plasters in common use are produced from ground gypsum rock by a process which removes most of the moisture from the rock to produce a powder that sets hard when mixed with water. Setting times are controlled by the use of retarding additives, which give each of the several types of plaster a setting time suitable to its use.

Gypsum plasters are intended for interior work only; they should not be used on permanently damp walls. They must not be remixed with water once they start to set.

PLASTER OF PARIS

This quick-setting non-retarded gypsum plaster gives off heat as it sets. It is white or pinkish, and is mixed to a creamy consistency with clean water. It is unsuitable for general plastering but good for casting, and can be used for repairs to decorative moldings.

BASE-COAT PLASTERS

In traditional plastering, the finish is built up in two or three successive coats. Base-coat plasters are used for all but the last coat.

Several types of base-coat plasters are available, some needing only to be mixed with water before application and others, which may need to be mixed with sand or other aggregate before they can be used effectively. Which type you choose may depend on the substrate, the specific job at hand, the desire for economy and the desired performance and working characteristics. It is crucial to read the package label to determine whether a particular formulation is suitable for the substrate or lath to which the plaster will be applied and to learn the best way to prepare the mixture.

Ordinary gypsum base-coat plaster, which must have sand or other aggregate added, is economical and suitable for most purposes. Wood-fiber base-coat plaster can be used with the addition of water only over wood, metal or gypsum lath, but must be mixed with sand for application over masonry. Wood-fiber plasters are about 25 percent lighter than sanded gypsum base coats and have greater fire resistance.

Special lightweight gypsum-based plasters, some pre-mixed with the aggregate (these are commonly known by the United States Gypsum Co. tradenames "Structo-base" and "Structo-lite") are higher in strength than conventional plasters. Portland cement-lime plaster is suitable for interior applications where a high-moisture condition prevails and for exterior stucco.

GAUGING PLASTER

Gauging plasters are designed to be mixed with lime putty and applied as a finish coat. Some grades are harder and more abrasion-resistant than others; which type is best-suited for a particular application may be determined by consulting with your supplier. In addition to blending gauging plaster with lime putty to improve workability, it may have aggregate added to roughen the finished texture.

FINISH-COAT PLASTER

Finish-coat plasters do not need to be mixed with lime putty. They are mixed with water and may be applied over compatible basecoats, gypsum lath and moisture-resistant-type gypsum wallboard. Some types are formulated for use over portland-cement-lime base coats for walls with moisture problems.

MOLDING PLASTER

With extremely fine grains and controlled set, molding plasters are preferred for casting and running ornamental trim and cornices. When used for running cornices with a template, the addition of lime putty may be necessary.

PATCHING PLASTER

Available in comparatively small packages, patching plasters are formulated for high bonding strength and are fast setting. Patching plasters are best suited to repairs of small areas.

FINISH LIME

Finish lime is added to plaster to provide bulk, plasticity and ease of spreading. It also helps to control the setting time. Conventional finish limes must be slaked, that is saturated with water for 16 to 24 hours to develop the desirable putty consistency and proper working characteristics. Specially processed types develop the necessary qualities immediately on being mixed with water.

OTHER ADDITIVES

Plaster retarders may be added to conventional plasters to slow drying and allow adequate working time. Accelerators may be added to speed hardening where conditions require it.

● **Avoiding old plaster**
Plaster may deteriorate if stored for more than two months, so suppliers try to make sure it is sold in rotation. The paper sacks in which plaster is supplied are usually date-stamped by the manufacturer. If you are buying from a self-service supplier, choose a sack with the latest date.

TYPES OF SURFACE

● **Providing a "key"**
Rake out mortar
joints to help plaster
and stucco grip.

A well-prepared ground is the first step to successful plastering. New surfaces of block or brickwork may need only dampening or priming with a bonding agent, depending on their absorbency. Old plastered surfaces needing repairs should be thoroughly checked. If the plaster is unsound, remove it to leave only stable material, then treat the surface and replaster the area.

Background preparation and absorbency

Brush down the surface of a masonry ground to remove loose particles, dust and efflorescent salts. Test the absorption of the masonry by splashing on water; if it stays wet, consider the surface normal—this means that it will only require light dampening with clean water prior to applying the plaster.

A dry background that absorbs the water immediately takes too much water from the plaster, making it difficult to work, and prevents it from setting properly, which can result in cracking. Soak the masonry with clean water applied with a brush.

High-absorbency surfaces

For very absorbent surfaces, such as aerated concrete blocks, prime the background with 1 part PVA bonding agent: 3 to 5 parts clean water. When dry, apply a bonding coat of 3 parts bonding agent: 1 part water. Apply the plaster when the bonding coat is tacky.

Low-absorbency surfaces

Prime low-absorption smooth brickwork or concrete with a solution of 1 part bonding agent: 3 to 5 parts water. Allow to dry. Apply a second coat of 3 to 5 parts bonding agent: 1 part water, and apply the plaster when tacky or allow it to dry for no more than 24 hours before plastering.

Non-absorbent surfaces

Glazed tiles and painted walls are considered non-absorbent and will require a coating of neat bonding agent to enable the plaster to stick. The plaster is applied while the agent is still wet. An alternative for glazed tiles is to apply a slurry of 2 parts sharp sand: 1 part cement mixed with a solution of 1 part bonding agent: 1 part water. Apply the slurry with a stiff-bristled brush to form a stippled coating. Allow to dry for 24 hours then apply the plaster.

The best option is to chip off the old tiles. Always remove loose tiles.

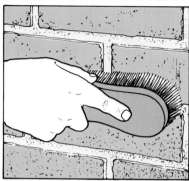
Remove loose particles with a stiff brush

Prime porous surfaces to control the suction

A bonding agent improves adhesion

Smooth tiles can be "keyed" with a slurry

MAKING FILLER AND MORTAR BOARDS

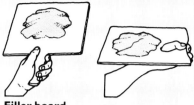

Filler board
You can make a useful board for mixing and working with plaster and compound from marine plywood. Cut out a 1-foot square with a projecting handle on one side, or make a thumb hole like an artist's palette. Seal the surface with a polyurethane varnish or apply a plastic laminate for a smooth finish.

Mortar board
Cut a piece of ½- or ¾-inch marine plywood approximately 3 feet square. Round off the corners and bevel the edges all round. Screw three lengths of 1-by-2 furring across the underside, spread equally apart. A smaller board, known as a spotboard, 2 feet square, can be made in a similar way.

Using a stand ▶
You will find it easier
to handle plaster with
the mix at table height.

Using a stand
A stand is used to support the mortar board at table height, about 30 inches from the ground. This enables the plaster to be picked up on a hawk by placing it under the edge of the board and drawing the plaster onto it.

Make a folding stand using 2-by-3 studs for the legs and 1-by-3 furring for the rails. Make one leg frame fit inside the other and bolt them securely together at the center.

A proprietary folding bench can be used to support the board instead of making a stand: grip the center support in the vise jaws.

With the ground prepared, the next step for the amateur plasterer is to make a good mix. It is best to mix your plaster close to the working place, since it can be messy. Also cover the floor with old newspapers and remember to wipe your feet when leaving the room.

A plaster that is well-mixed to the right consistency will be easier to apply. Use a plastic bucket to measure the cement, lime and sand, or plaster accurately. For large quantities of plaster, multiply the number of bucket measures. For small quantities, just use half-bucket measures or less.

Old, hard plaster stuck to your equipment can shorten the setting time and reduce the strength of the newly mixed plaster. Do not try to re-work plaster that has begun to set by adding more water: discard it and make a fresh batch. Mix only as much plaster as you will need. For larger areas, mix as much as you can apply in about twenty minutes—judge this by practice.

BONDING AGENTS

Bonding agents modify the suction of the ground or improve the adhesion of the plastering. When used, the base-coat plaster should not exceed ⅜ inches in thickness. If you need to build up the thickness, scratch the surface to provide an extra key, and allow at least 24 hours between coats.

Bonding agents can be mixed with plaster or sand and cement to fill cracks. First brush away any loose particles and then apply a solution of 1 part agent: 3 to 5 parts water with a brush.

Mix the plaster or sand and cement with 1 part bonding agent: 3 parts water to a stiff mix. Apply the filler with a trowel, pressing it well into the crack.

Wash tools and brushes thoroughly in clean water when you are finished. It may be necessary to rinse out the brushes as the work progresses on a large job.

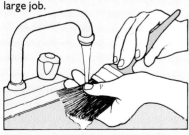

Wash agent from brushes before it sets

Base-coat plasters

Mix base-coat plasters on a mortar board (see opposite). For sanded plasters, measure out each of the materials and thoroughly dry-mix them with a shovel or trowel for small quantities (▷). Make a well in the heaped plaster and pour in some clean water. Turn in the plaster, adding water to produce a thick, creamy consistency.

Just add water to pre-mixed gypsum plaster (which already contains an aggregate). Mix them on the board in the same way. Always wash down the board after use.

You can mix small quantities of pre-mixed plaster in a bucket. Pour the plaster into the water and stir to a creamy consistency; 2½ pounds of plaster will need about 1½ pints of water.

Finish plaster

Mix finish plaster in a clean plastic bucket. Add the powder to the water. Pour no more than 4 pints of water into the bucket. Sprinkle the plaster into the water and stir it with a broad length of wood to a thick, creamy consistency. Tip the plaster out onto a clean, damp mortar board ready for use. Wash the bucket out with clean water before the plaster sets in it.

SEE ALSO

Details for: ▷

Builder's tools	75-76
Applying plaster	36
Repairing plasterwork	37

COVERAGE OF GAUGED-LIME FINISH PLASTERS*

Plaster product	Ratio of mix			Approximate coverage in sq. yds. per 100 lbs. of plaster
	Lime	Gauging	Sand	
Standard gauging plasters	2	1	–	19.5
	2	1	8	14
Structo-Gauge†	1	1	–	19
	2	1	–	21.5
Keenes cement	2	1	8	13.5
	1	2	–	18.5
	1	2	8	13.5

* Mix ratios and approximate coverages are based on information contained in Gypsum Construction Handbook, 2nd edition, published by the United States Gypsum Co. † Structo-Gauge is a USG trademark.

COVERAGE OF BASE-COAT PLASTERS*

Plaster product	Mix	Ratio: aggregate by vol./plaster by weight	Approximate coverage in sq. yds. per 100 lbs. of plaster		
			Gypsum lath	Metal lath	Unit masonry
Standard gypsum base-coat plasters	Sand	2.0–3.0	10.5	5.75	9.25
	Perlite	2.0–3.0	9.25	4.5	7.5
	Vermiculite	2.0–3.0	9	–	8.25
Wood fiber	Neat	–	6.75	2.5	5.25
	Sand	1.0	6.75	3.5	5.25
Structo-Lite†	Regular	–	7	3.75	6.75
Structo-Base†	Sand	2.0–3.0	8.25	5	7.6

* Mix ratios and approximate coverages are based on information contained in Gypsum Construction Handbook, 2nd edition, published by the United States Gypsum Co. † Structo-Life and Structo-Base are USG trademarks.

Plaster fillers

Pour out a small heap of the powder on to a small board, make a hollow in its center and pour in water. Stir the mix to a creamy thickness; if it seems too runny add more powder. Use a rather drier mix for filling deeper holes.

APPLYING PLASTER

To the beginner, plastering can seem an overwhelming job, yet it has only two basic requirements: that the plaster should stick well to its ground and that it should be brought to a smooth, flat finish. Good preparation, the careful choice of plaster and working with the right tools should guarantee good adhesion of the material, but the ability to achieve the smooth, flat surface will come only after some practice. Most of the plasterer's tools (◁) are rather specialized and unlikely to be found in the ordinary tool kit, but their cost may prove economical in the long term if you are planning several jobs.

Problems to avoid

Uneven surfaces

Many amateurs tackle plastering jobs, large or small, planning to rub the surface down level when it has set. This approach is very dusty and laborious, and invariably produces a poor result. If a power sander is used, the dust is unpleasant to work in and permeates other parts of the house, making more work. It is better to try for a good surface as you put the plaster on, using wide-bladed tools to spread the material evenly. Ridges left by the corners of the trowel or knife can be carefully shaved down afterwards with the knife—not with abrasive paper.

When covering a large area with finishing plaster, it is not always easy to see if the surface is flat as well as smooth. Look obliquely across the wall or shine a light across it from one side to detect any irregularities.

Crazing

Fine cracks in finished plaster may be due to a sand-and-cement undercoat still drying out, and therefore shrinking. Such an undercoat must be fully dry before the plaster goes on, though if the plaster surface is sound, the fine cracks can be wallpapered over.

Top-coat and undercoat plaster can also crack if made to dry out too fast. Never heat plaster to dry it out.

Loss of strength

Gypsum and cement set chemically when mixed with water. If they dry out before the chemical set takes place, they do not develop their full strength and they become fragile. If this happens it may be necessary to strip the wall and replaster it.

PLASTERING TECHNIQUES

Picking up

Hold the edge of the hawk below the mortar board and scrape a manageable amount of plaster onto the hawk, using the trowel (**1**). Take no more than a trowelful to start with.

Tip the hawk towards you and in one movement cut away about half of the plaster with the trowel, scraping and lifting it off the hawk and onto the face of the trowel (**2**).

1 Load the hawk   **2 Lift off the plaster**

Application

Hold the loaded trowel horizontally but tilted at an angle to the face of the wall (**1**). Apply the plaster with a vertical upward stroke, pressing firmly so that plaster is fed to the wall. Flatten the angle of the trowel as you go (**2**) but never let its whole face come into contact with the plaster since suction can pull it off the wall again.

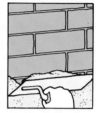

1 Tilt the trowel   **2 Apply the plaster**

Leveling up

Build a slight extra thickness of plaster with the trowel, applying it as evenly as possible. Use the rule (◁) to level the surface, starting at the bottom of the wall, the rule held against original plaster or wooden screeds nailed on at either side. Work the rule upwards while moving it from side to side, then lift it carefully away and the surplus plaster with it. Fill in any hollows with more plaster from the trowel, then level again. Let the plaster stiffen before a final smoothing with the trowel.

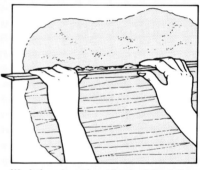

Work the rule up the wall to level the surface

Finishing

You can apply the finishing coat to a gypsum-plaster undercoat as soon as it sets. Cement-based sanded plaster must dry thoroughly, but dampen its surface for suction before finish-plastering. The gray face of gypsum lath is finished immediately and is not wetted.

Apply the finish with a plasterer's trowel as described above, spreading it evenly, no more than $1/16$- to $1/8$-inch, judging by eye, as screeds are not used. To gypsum board apply two coats to build a $3/16$-inch thickness.

As the plaster stiffens, brush or lightly spray it with water, then trowel the surface to consolidate it and produce a smooth matte finish. Do not press hard or overwork the surface. Remove surplus water with a sponge.

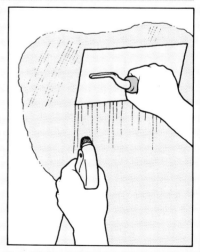

Spray plaster occasionally as you smooth it

REINFORCING A CORNER

When damage to a corner extends along most of the edge, you can reinforce the repair plasterwork with a metal corner bead (**1**). As well as strengthening and protecting the new corner, it will speed up the repair work because it cuts out the need to use a board as a guide. You can obtain the corner bead from a good builders' supply or DIY store.

Cut the beading to the required length with scissors or a hacksaw. It has a galvanized protective coating, and the cut ends must be sealed with a metal primer or bituminous paint.

Cut back the old plaster from the damaged edge, wet the brickwork and apply patches of undercoat plaster at each side of the corner. Press the expanded metal wings of the bead into the plaster patches (**2**), using your straightedge to align its outer nose with both original plaster surfaces or checking the bead for evenness with a builder's level. Allow the plaster to set.

Build up the undercoat as before (**3**), but this time scrape it back to 1/16-inch below the old finished level.

Apply the finishing coat, using the bead as a level to achieve flush surfaces. Take care not to damage the beading's galvanized coating with your trowel; rust can come through later and stain wallcoverings. To be on the safe side, you can brush metal primer over the new corner before decorating.

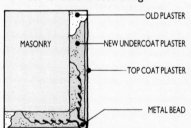

OLD PLASTER
MASONRY
NEW UNDERCOAT PLASTER
TOP COAT PLASTER
METAL BEAD

1 Section through a repaired corner

2 Set in plaster

3 Trim undercoat back

REPAIRING PLASTERWORK

Every decorator at some time will have to fill small holes and cracks with plaster or filler as part of normal patching preparations—these jobs should present few problems. But once you start tackling more ambitious jobs, such as removing fireplaces and taking down walls, you will need to develop some of the professional plasterer's skills in order to handle jobs of this magnitude.

Plastering over a fireplace

A bricked-in fireplace provides an area large enough to give the amateur good practice without being overwhelmed. Jobs like this can be done with a one-coat plaster, or with an undercoat plaster followed by a top coat of finishing plaster.

Using a one-coat plaster
Prepare the background by cutting away any loose plaster above and around the brickwork. Remove dust and loose particles with a stiff brush.

Mix the plaster in a tub according to the maker's instructions.

Dampen the background with clean water and place a strip of hardboard below the work area to help you to pick up dropped plaster cleanly.

Tip the mixed plaster onto a dampened mortar board, then scoop some onto a hawk, and with a trowel (or the spreader provided) apply the plaster to the brickwork.

Work in the sequence shown (**1**), starting at the bottom of each section and spreading the plaster vertically. Work each area in turn, blending the edge of one into the next to build up a slight extra thickness, then level with a rule (▷). Fill any hollows and level again.

Leave the plaster to stiffen for about 45 minutes, when firm finger pressure leaves no impression, then lightly dampen the surface with a close-textured plastic sponge.

Wet the trowel or spreader and give the plaster a smooth finish, using firm pressure vertically and horizontally and keeping the tool wet.

Let the plaster dry thoroughly, for about six weeks, before decorating.

Two-coat plastering
Apply undercoat and finishing coat plasters as described above, scraping the undercoat back to allow for the thickness of the finishing coat.

Repairing a chipped corner

When part of the outside corner of a plastered wall has broken away to show the brickwork behind, you can rebuild it with either one- or two-coat plaster. Use a 4-inch-wide board as a guide to get the corner straight.

With a bolster (▷), cut the plaster back from the damaged edge to reveal about 4 inches of the brickwork.

For two-coat plaster, place the guide board against the old plasterwork, set back about 1/8-inch from the surface of the plaster on the other side of the corner (**1**). Fasten the board to the brickwork temporarily with masonry nails through the mortar joints, placing them well away from the corner.

Mix up the undercoat plaster, wet the brickwork and edge of the old plaster, then fill the one side of the corner flush with the edge of the board but not the wall (**2**). Scratch-key the new plaster with the trowel.

When the plaster is stiff, remove the board, pulling it straight from the wall to prevent the new plaster breaking away. The exposed edge represents the finished surface, so scrape it back about 1/8-inch with the trowel and straight-edge (**3**) to allow for the top coat.

For such a job, a professional would simply hold the board over the new repair and fill the second side of the corner immediately. But this leaves only one hand to lift and apply the plaster, a difficult trick for the amateur. An easier, though slower, method is to let the new plaster harden, then nail the board through it before applying and keying fresh plaster as before (**4**). Or, if the new plaster is set hard, you can use the scraped edge as a guide.

Let the undercoat set, then nail the board to the wall as before, but this time set it flush with the corner and level off with finishing plaster. Dampen the undercoat if necessary, to help the top coat to stick.

When both sides are firm, polish the new plaster with a wet trowel, rounding over the sharp edge slightly, then leave it to dry out.

If you choose to carry out the repair with a one-coat plaster you must set the board flush with the corner before applying the material.

SEE ALSO

Details for: ▷
Builder's tools   75-76
Background preparation   34

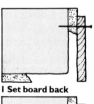

1 Plastering sequence
Divide the area into manageable portions and apply the plaster in the sequence shown.

1 Set board back

2 Fill flush with board

3 Scrape back edge

4 Fill second side

PATCHING A WALLBOARD CEILING

A misplaced foot in the attic, a roof leak not attended to, a leaking water pipe—any of these can cause damage to a ceiling. Fortunately the damage is usually of a localized kind that can be simply patch-repaired.

Before starting work, turn off the electricity at the service panel. The next job is to check the direction in which the ceiling joists run and determine whether there is any electrical wiring close by the damaged area. If the damaged ceiling is below a floor, such an inspection can usually be carried out from above, by raising a floorboard. An alternative is to knock an inspection hole through the center of the damage with a hammer. You will find that it is possible to look along the void with the help of a flashlight and a mirror (1).

1 Use a mirror and flashlight to inspect a void

Close the damaged area, mark out a square or rectangle on the ceiling. Cut away an area of the wallboard slightly larger than the damage, working up to the sides of the nearest joists (2). Use a wallboard saw or, if there is wiring nearby, a utility knife, which will just penetrate the thickness of the wallboard.

Cut and toenail 2-by-4 cross-braces between the joists at the ends of the cutout, with half of their thickness projecting beyond the cut edges of the wallboard (3).

Nail 1-by-2 furring to the sides of the joists flush with their bottom edges (4).

Cut your wallboard patch to fit the opening with a 1/8-inch gap all around, and nail it to the 2-by-4 and furring. Fill and tape over the joints to give a flush surface (◁).

Minor damage
Repair minor damage to wallboard as when preparing to decorate.

2 Cut an opening

3 Nail in cross-braces

4 Nail in furring

REPAIRING LATH AND PLASTER

When the plaster of a lath and plaster wall deteriorates with age it can lose its grip on the laths because its key has gone. This may show itself as a swelling, perhaps with some cracking. It will make a hollow sound if tapped and will yield when it is pressed. The loose plaster should be replaced.

Repairing a wall

Cut out the plaster with a cold chisel and hammer (1). If the laths are sound you can replaster over them. Dampen the wooden laths and plaster edges (2) around the hole and apply a one-coat plaster with a plasterer's trowel, pressing it firmly between the laths as you coat them (3). Build up the coating flush with the surrounding plaster and level it with a rule. Let the plaster stiffen and smooth it with a damp sponge and a trowel. Another option is to apply it in two coats. Scratch-key the first coat and let it set (4), then apply the second and finish as before.

For large repairs, use the two coats of pre-mixed lightweight bonding undercoat, or metal-lathing plaster, followed by a finishing plaster. For a small patch repair, use joint compound, pressing it on and between laths.

If laths are damaged, cut them out and replace them, or cover the studs with wallboard and finish with plaster. When using wallboard, nail it in the opening with the grey side towards you.

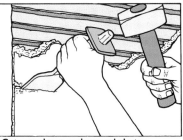

1 Cut away loose or damaged plaster

2 Dampen edges of old sound plaster

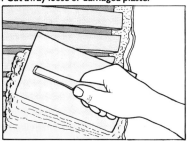

3 Apply plaster pressing it between laths

4 Scratch key the undercoat

Repairing a ceiling

A water leak above a lath and plaster ceiling will cause localized damage to the plaster. Repair the ceiling with metal-lathing plaster, finishing with a top-coat gypsum plaster (◁).

Carefully cut back the plaster to sound material. Dampen the background and apply the undercoat (1). Don't build up a full thickness. Key the surface and let it set. Give the ceiling a second coat, scrape it back 1/8-inch below the surface and lightly key it. When set, finish-coat the ceiling using a plasterer's trowel (2).

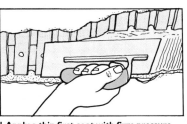

1 Apply a thin first coat with firm pressure

2 Level top coat over keyed undercoat

PLASTERING A WALL

The plastering of a complete wall is usually not necessary in many households. Any new work is much easier to carry out with wallboard (▷), but there are times when repairs are needed due to moisture problems or alterations such as moving doorways, leaving large areas to be plastered. This repair can be done by the non-professional. The key to success is to divide the wall into manageable areas (see below). Some previous practice, for example when patching up decayed plaster, is helpful to do the job without errors.

Applying the plaster

Using the face of the plasterer's trowel, scrape several trowel-loads of plaster onto the hawk and start undercoat plastering at the top of the wall, holding the trowel at an angle to the face of the wall and applying the plaster with vertical strokes. Work from right to left if you are right-handed and from left to right if you are left-handed (see below).

Using firm pressure to guarantee good adhesion, apply first a thin layer and then follow this with more plaster, building up the required thickness. If the final thickness of the plaster needs to be more than ⅜-inch, key the surface with a scratcher and let it set, then apply a second coat to finish the surface.

Fill in the area between two screed strips. It is not necessary to work tight up against them. Level the surface by running the rule upwards, laid across the screeds, and working it from side to side as you go. Fill in any hollows and then level the plaster again. Scratch the surface lightly to provide a key for the finishing coat and let the plaster set. Work along the wall in this way, then remove the screeds and fill the gaps they have left between the plastered areas, again leveling with the rule.

With gypsum plasters, the finishing coat can be applied as soon as the undercoat is set. Cement undercoats must be left to dry for at least 24 hours because of shrinkage (▷), then wetted when the top coat is applied.

The order for applying plaster

UNDERCOAT
SCREEDS
TOP COAT

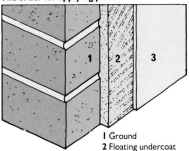

Two-coat plastering

1 Ground
2 Floating undercoat
3 Finishing top coat

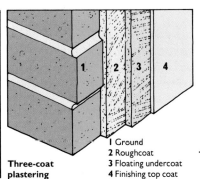

Three-coat plastering

1 Ground
2 Roughcoat
3 Floating undercoat
4 Finishing top coat

PREPARING TO PLASTER

In addition to the plastering tools you need a level and some lengths of ⅜-inch wood strip. The wood strips—known as screeds—are for nailing to the wall, to act as guides when it comes to leveling the plaster. Professional plasterers form plaster screeds by applying bands of undercoat plaster to the required thickness. These may be vertical or horizontal.

Prepare the ground (▷) and fasten the wooden screeds vertically to the wall with masonry nails. Driving the nails home will make it easier for you to work the trowel, but it can also make it more difficult to remove the screeds afterwards. The screeds should be spaced no more than 2 feet apart. Use the level to get them truly even, shimming them out with strips of hardboard or wood as necessary.

Mix the undercoat plaster to a thick, creamy consistency and measure out two bucketfuls to begin with, although you can increase this to larger amounts when you become a little more proficient at working with the material.

Finishing

Cover the undercoat with a thin layer of finishing plaster, working from top to bottom and from left to right (see left) using even, vertical strokes. Work with the trowel held at a slight angle so that only its one edge is touching.

Make sweeping horizontal strokes to level the surface further. You can try using the rule in getting the initial surface even, but you may risk dragging the finish coat off. Use the trowel to smooth out any slight ripples.

Wet the trowel and work over the surface with firm pressure to consolidate the plaster, and as it sets, trowel it to produce a smooth matt finish. Don't overwork it, and wipe away any plaster slurry that appears with a damp sponge.

The walls should be left to dry out for several weeks before decorating.

◀ **Plaster layers**
Plaster is applied in layers to build up a smooth level surface. Two or three coats may be used.

Level the screeds
Shim out the screed strips at the fastening points as required.

GYPSUM WALLBOARD

STORING AND CUTTING GYPSUM WALLBOARD

Wallboard provides a relatively quick and simple method of finishing the rough structural materials of walls and ceilings. It is easy to cut and apply, with adhesives or mechanical fasteners.

A range of gypsum wallboard products is available from builders' supplies. The boards are all based on a core of gypsum plaster covered on both sides with a strong paper liner. They may have a grey paper facing or green, indicating they are moisture-resistant. As well as coming in a range of thicknesses and sheet sizes, the boards can also have tapered or beveled edges. Wallboard joints are usually finished with tape and compound and then decorated. In some cases, a skim coat of plaster is applied to the wallboard before decoration.

Wallboard is fragile, having very little structural strength, and the sheets are quite heavy, so always get someone to help you carry a sheet, and hold it on its edge. To carry it flat is to run a serious risk of breaking it.

Manufacturers and suppliers of the material store it flat in stacks, but this is usually inconvenient at home and is anyway not necessary for a small number of sheets. Instead store them on edge, leaning them slightly against a wall, their outer faces together to protect them. Place the sheets down carefully to avoid damaging their edges.

Cutting wallboard
Wallboard can be cut with a saw or with a stiff-bladed craft knife.

The sheet must be supported, face side up, on lengths of wood laid across saw horses and with the cutting line marked on it with the aid of a straightedge. When sawing, the saw should be held at a shallow angle to the surface of the wallboard, and if the cutoff is a large one, a helper should support it to prevent it breaking away towards the end of the cut.

When cutting wallboard with a knife, cut well into the material following a straightedge, snap the board along the cutting line over a length of wood and cut through the paper liner on the other side to separate the pieces.

To make openings in wallboard for electrical and other fittings, you can use a keyhole saw, a power jigsaw or a craft knife.

Remove any ragged paper after cutting by rubbing down the cut edges with an abrasive paper.

Tapered edge

Square edge

Beveled edge

Types of edges
Ordinary wallboard used as the primary wall finish have tapered edges to facilitate the building up of compound to create a flush surface. Gypsum bases and lath typically have square edges. Pre-decorated wallboards, which are not finished with compound, have beveled edges to create a pleasing V-joint pattern when installed.

GYPSUM PANEL PRODUCTS

GYPSUM PANEL TYPES AND USES	THICKNESSES (inches)	WIDTHS (inches)	LENGTHS (feet)	EDGE FINISHES
Standard wallboard				
This material is generally used to finish walls and ceilings. The long edges of the panels are tapered to accommodate the built-up layers of tape and compound used to finish joints. Available in a variety of thicknesses, $\frac{5}{8}$- and $\frac{1}{2}$-in. panels are typically used for single-layer applications direct to studs, while $\frac{3}{8}$-in. is normally used over existing wall finishes; $\frac{1}{4}$-in. wallboard is generally used in multi-layer applications for sound control and for curved surfaces with short radii.	$\frac{1}{4}$ $\frac{3}{8}$, $\frac{1}{2}$, $\frac{5}{8}$	48 48	8 8, 9, 10, 12, 14	Tapered
Water-resistant gypsum panels				
With a specially formulated gypsum-asphalt core and chemically-treated face and back papers, this material is recommended for direct application to studs in bathrooms, powder rooms and utility rooms to combat moisture penetration. Suitable as base for ceramic tile and plastic-faced wall panels.	$\frac{1}{2}$, $\frac{5}{8}$	48	8, 10, 12	Tapered
Predecorated gypsum panels				
These are standard wallboard panels that have a wide range of factory-applied vinyl and fabric facings. Long edges of panels are beveled to form a shallow V-groove at joints.	$\frac{1}{2}$	48	8, 9, 10	Beveled
Gypsum-base panels				
Gypsum bases are used in conjunction with proprietary veneer finishes to create the beauty of a plaster finish with less labor, weight and residual moisture.	$\frac{1}{2}$, $\frac{5}{8}$	48	8, 10, 12, 14	Square
Gypsum lath				
This product category includes a variety of panel products specially designed as a ground for standard plaster base coats and finishes.	$\frac{3}{8}$, $\frac{1}{2}$	16, 24	4, 8	Square

APPLYING WALLBOARD

Wallboard can be nailed directly to the framework of a stud partition or to furring strips that are fastened to a solid masonry wall. It can also be bonded straight onto solid walls with an adhesive.

The boards may be fitted horizontally if it is more economical to do so, but generally they are placed vertically. All of the edges should be supported.

When finishing a ceiling and walls, cover the ceiling before you finish the wall.

Methods of fastening wallboard

Nailing to a stud partition
Partition walls may simply be plain room-dividers or they may include doorways. When you are finishing a plain wall, you should work from one corner when you start hanging the board, but where there is a doorway, you may want to work away from it towards the corners.

Starting from a corner
Hold the first board in position. Mark and scribe the edge that meets the adjacent wall if this is necessary (▷), then nail or screw the board into position, securing it to all the frame members (see right).

Fasten the rest of the boards in place, working across the partition. Butt the edges of tapered-edged boards, but leave a gap of about ⅛-inch between boards that are going to be coated with tape and compound.

If necessary, scribe the edge of the last board to fit the end corner before nailing it into place.

Cut a baseboard, mitering the joints at the corners or scribing the ends of the new board to the original (▷). Fit the baseboard.

Starting from a doorway
Position the first board flush with the door stud and mark the position of the underside of the door's head member on the edge of the board. Between the mark on the board's edge and its top edge, cut out a strip 1-inch wide. Reposition the board and fasten it in place, nailing it to all frame members (see right).

Fasten the rest of the boards in place, working towards the corner. Butt the edges of tapered-edge boards but leave a ⅛-inch gap all around boards which are to be coated afterwards with tape and compound.

If necessary, scribe the last board to fit any irregularities in the corner (▷) before fastening it in place.

Cover the rest of the wall on the other side of the doorway in the same way, starting by cutting a 1-inch strip from the first board between its top edge and a mark indicating the lower side of the door's head member.

Cut a wallboard panel to go above the doorway, butting into the cutouts in the boards on each side of the door. Sandpaper away the ragged edges of paper before fitting the panel.

When all of the wallboard is in place, fill and finish the joints (▷). Cut and fit door jambs (▷) and cover the edges with a casing.

Cut and fit baseboards (▷), nailing through the wallboard into studs underneath.

WALLBOARD NAILS

Use special galvanized drywall nails of lengths appropriate to the thickness of the wallboard, as shown in the table below.

Space the nails about 12 inches apart and place them not less than ⅜-inch from the paper-covered edge and ½-inch from the cut ends. Drive the nails in straight so that they sink just below the surface without tearing through the paper lining.

Board thickness	Nail length
⅜"	1¼"
½"	1⅝"
⅝"	1⅝"

Note that 1¼-inch drywall screws are adequate for most single-layer applications. Use longer screws when applying wallboard in two layers or over existing wall finish.

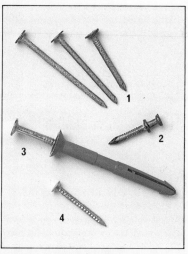

Types of nail used with wallboard

Drywall nails
1 Galvanized nails
2 Double-headed nail
3 Nailable plug
4 Ring nail

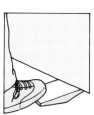

Using a footlifter
Cut the board about ⅝-in. below room height to clear the rootlifter, a simple tool that holds the board against the ceiling leaving both hands free for nailing. You can make one from a 3-in.-wide wood block.

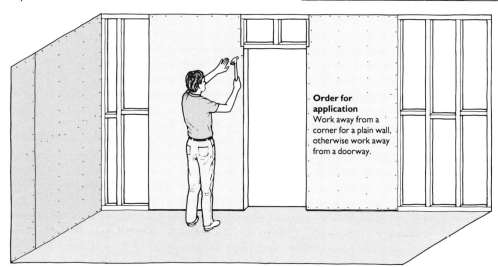

Order for application
Work away from a corner for a plain wall, otherwise work away from a doorway.

● **Distances between stud centers**
When providing new studs, it is cheaper to use ½-in. thick board on studs set 24 in. apart. Maximum distance between stud centers: for ⅜-in. board—16 in., for ½- and ⅝-in. board—24-in.

SCRIBING WALLBOARD

If the inner edge of the first sheet of wallboard butts against an uneven wall, or its other edge does not fall on the center of the stud, the board must be scribed to fit.

Scribing the first board

Try the first board in position **(1)**. The case shown is of an uneven wall pushing the wallboard beyond the studs at the other edge of the wallboard, and of the problem encountered when the end stud in a partition is not set at the normal spacing.

Move and reposition the board **(2)** so that its inner edge lies on the center of the stud and tack it into place with drywall nails driven partway into the intermediate studs. Before temporarily tacking the board, make sure it is set at the right height by using the footlifter. With a pencil and a guide (cut the width of the board), trace a line down the face of the board, copying the contour of the wall. It is essential to keep the guide level while doing this.

Trim the waste away from the scribed edge, following the line, replace the board in the corner and fasten it with nails or screws **(3)**.

Scribing the last board

Temporarily nail the board to be scribed over the last fixed board **(4)**, making sure that their edges lie flush.

Using a guide and a pencil as above, trace a pencil line down the face of the board, carefully keeping the guide level.

Remove the marked board, cut away the scribed area to cut it to size and nail it into place **(5)**.

1 Try the first board in the corner

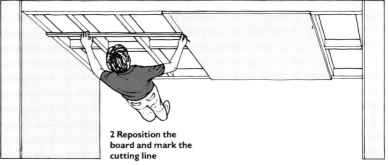

2 Reposition the board and mark the cutting line

3 Cut the board to size and nail in place

4 Temporarily nail and mark out the last board to fit

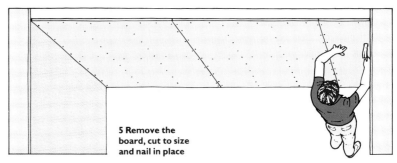

5 Remove the board, cut to size and nail in place

SOLID WALL FURRING

Wallboard cannot be nailed directly to solid masonry walls. One-by-two lengths of wood known as furring strips are used to provide a good basis for the nails and to counter any unevenness of the wall surface. These strips should be treated with a wood preservative.

You can cover sound old plaster but if it is in poor condition, strip it back to the brickwork. If the failure of the original plaster was caused by moisture, it must be treated and if possible allowed to dry out before refinishing.

Fit any plumbing pipe runs, electrical conduit or cable to the wall before the furring is applied to conceal them.

Marking out

Use a straightedge to mark the position of the furring strips on the wall with vertical chalk lines. The lines should be placed at 16-inch or 24-inch centers according to the width and thickness of the wallboard being used, bearing in mind that sheets of wallboard must meet on the center lines of the furring strips. Work away from any door or window opening and allow for the thickness of the furring and wallboard at the moldings (▷).

Fastening the furring

Cut the required number of furring strips from 1-by-2 or 1-by-3 lumber. The vertical strips should be cut slightly shorter than the height of the wall. The horizontal strips should be cut to run along the tops and bottoms of the vertical ones and any short vertical lengths above and below openings (see below).

Nail the vertical furring strips on first, setting their bottom ends about 4 inches above the floor. Fasten them with masonry nails or cut nails, with the face of each strip level with the guide line (see right), and check with the straightedge and level that they are also flat and plumb, shimming them out if necessary.

Now nail the horizontal strips across the tops and bottoms of the vertical members, shimming them to the same level if necessary.

Fastening the wallboard

To fasten wallboard to furring strips, follow the same procedure as described for nailing to a stud partition (▷), except that in this case the boards at the sides of doors and windows do not need to be notched to receive panels above or below the openings.

The procedure for filling and finishing the joints between the sheets of wallboard is also identical.

Cut the baseboard to length and nail it through the wallboard to the bottom horizontal furring strip, although if it is a high baseboard of the type used in old, high-ceilinged houses, it can be nailed to the vertical strips.

LEVELING THE FURRING STRIPS

Masonry walls are often uneven and this must be taken into account when fastening the furring if the lining is to finish straight and flat.

To check if the wall is flat hold a long straightedge horizontally against it at different levels. If it proves to be uneven, mark the vertical chalk line already drawn on the wall that is the closest to the highest point **(1)**.

Hold a straight furring strip vertically on the marked chalk line, keeping it plumb with a straightedge and strip level, then mark the floor **(2)** where the face of the strip falls. Draw a straight guide line across the floor **(3)**, passing through this mark and meeting the walls on each end at right angles.

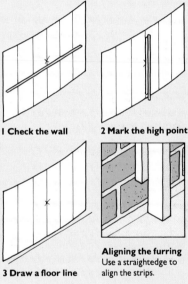

1 Check the wall

2 Mark the high point

3 Draw a floor line

Aligning the furring
Use a straightedge to align the strips.

SEE ALSO

Details for: ▷
Applying wallboard 41
Angles and
openings 45

**Using furring strips:
Order of working**
1 Mark furring positions.
2 Fasten vertical strips.
3 Fasten horizontal strips.
4 Fasten short pieces over doors and windows and offset the short vertical ones.
5 Nail boards in place working away from a door or window.

BONDING TO A SOLID WALL

As an alternative to using furring strips on a solid wall as a basis for wallboard, tapered-edged wallboard can be bonded directly to the wall with dabs of plaster or an adhesive. Special pads are produced for leveling up the wall, but squares cut from remnants of the wallboard itself can be used.

The pads are first bonded to the wall in lines that substitute for furring, then dabs of plaster are applied between the lines of pads and the wallboard is temporarily nailed to the pads while the plaster sets. The special double-headed nails are then removed.

Ordinary wallboard may be used with this technique. The wall must first be prepared in the usual way (◁).

I **Bond pads to the wall and level them**

Bonding the pads

Set out vertical chalk lines on the wall 16 inches apart, working from one corner or from a doorway or window opening (see below).

Draw a horizontal line 9 inches from the ceiling, one 4 inches from the floor and another centred between them. If the wall is more than 8 feet high, divide the space between the top and bottom equally with two lines. Place the pads where horizontal and vertical lines intersect.

Using a level and a straightedge almost at the height of the wall, check the wall at each vertical line, noting high spots at the intersections of the lines.

Bond a pad on the most prominent intersection point, using a bonding-coat plaster or a proprietary plaster adhesive, and press it in place to leave not less than $1/8$-inch of adhesive behind it (**1**). The rest of the pads are leveled up to the first one with plaster or adhesive.

Bond and plumb the other pads on the same vertical line, then complete a second vertical row two lines from the first. Check these pads for level vertically, then diagonally with the first row. Work across the wall in this way, then bond remaining pads on the other intersections. Allow two hours to set.

2 **Apply thick dabs of plaster between pads**

Bonding the wallboard

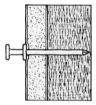

Double-headed nails
Use these special nails to temporarily hold the board while the plaster adhesive sets.

Apply thick dabs of adhesive or bonding plaster to the wall with a trowel (**2**) over an area for one board at a time. Space them 3 inches apart vertically and do not overlap the area of the next board. Press the board firmly against the pads so that the plaster spreads out behind it. Use the straightedge to press it evenly and the footlifter to position it.

Check the alignment, then fasten the board with double-headed nails driven through it into the pads round the edge. Bond the next board in the same way, butting it to the first, and work on across the wall, scribing the last board into the corner (◁). When the plaster has set, remove the nails with pliers or a claw hammer, protecting the wallboard surface (**3**).

Work around angles and openings (see opposite) and when all surfaces are covered, fill and finish the joints (◁).

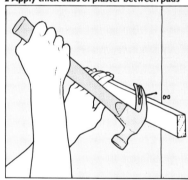

3 **Pull out the nails when plaster is set**

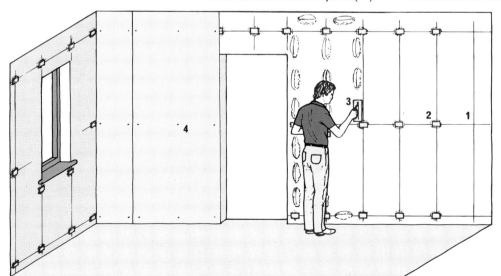

The bonding method order of working
1 Mark pad positions.
2 Stick the pads to the wall.
3 Apply dabs of plaster.
4 Place wallboard and temporarily nail. Remove nails when plaster is set.

WINDOW OPENINGS

Cut the wallboard linings for the window reveals and soffit to length and width. These are put into place before the wall finish. Their front edges should line up with the faces of the wall pads or furring strips.

Apply evenly spaced dabs of plaster adhesive to the back of the soffit lining, press it into place (1) and prop it there while the plaster adhesive sets. If the lining covers a wide span also use a wooden board to support it. Fit the reveal linings in the same way (2).

Working away from the window, bond the wall linings so that the paper-covered edge of the board laps the cut edge of the reveal lining.

The panels for above and below the window are cut and fitted last. Sandpaper off any rough edges of paper and leave a 1/8-inch gap for filling.

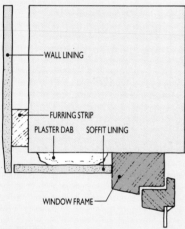

1 Soffit lining
Bond a soffit lining with dabs of plaster and prop in place until set.

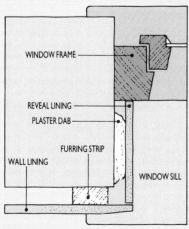

2 Reveal lining
Like the soffit lining, cut and bond the reveal so the wall lining overlaps its cut edge.

ANGLES AND OPENINGS

Inside corner

Fasten wooden furring strips or bonded gypsum board pads close to the corner. Whenever possible always place the cut edges of the wallboard into an inside corner.

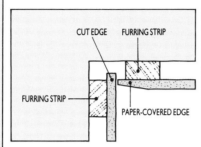

Inside corner
Set cut edges into the angle.

Outside corner

Attach furring strips of gypsum board pads and close to the corner as possible. Use screws and wall plugs to attach the furring so as to prevent the corner breaking away. Apply metal corner bead over the joint and finish with three coats of compound.

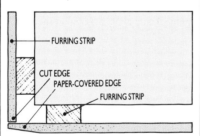

Outside corner
A paper-covered edge should lap the other edge.

Door openings

The reveals of doorways in exterior walls should be treated in the same way as described for window openings (see left).

In the case of interior door openings, screw wooden furring strips or bond gypsum board pads level with the edge of the blockwork, then nail or bond the wallboard into place.

Fit a new door jamb or modify the old one if necessary and cover the joint with a casing.

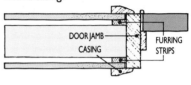

Electrical outlets

Depending on the type of fitting, build a chase or shim out the mounting box for an electrical switch or socket outlet so that it finishes flush with the face of the wallboard lining. Screw short lengths of furring strip at each side of the box, or apply dabs of adhesive or plaster for pads if using the bonding method (see opposite).

Cut the opening for the box before mounting the board. If you find it difficult to mark the opening accurately by transferring measurements to the board, remove the fixture from the box and take an impression of it by placing the board in position and pressing it against the box.

Mount the wallboard panel in place and replace the electrical fixture.

SEE ALSO

Details for:▷
Finishing wallboard   46–47

Interior door opening
Fit a new jamb or widen the old one and cover the joint between the jamb and wallboard with a casing.

Electrical outlets
Build a chase or shim out the mounting box to set it flush with the wallboard.

Angle treatments: Order of working
1 Fit soffit lining.
2 Fit reveal lining.
3 Fit boards working away from window.
4 Fit panels over and under window.
5 Fit boards working away from doorway.
6 Cut and fit panel over doorway.
7 Cut openings for electrical fixtures as they occur.

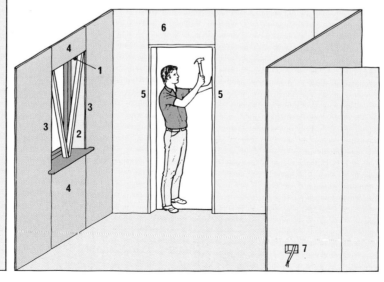

FINISHING WALLBOARD

All of the joints between boards and the indentations left by nailing must be filled and smoothed before the surface of the wallboard is ready for direct decoration.

To finish wallboard for applying decoration, you will need filler, joint tape and a variety of taping knives. The technique is not difficult.

Tools and materials

To finish wallboard joints, you will need joint compound—a premixed plaster-like substance that is available in 5-gallon pails, joint tape and a variety of joint knives ranging in width from 3 to 10 inches. In addition to these items, you will need a hawk, which is used to hold the compound and from which you load the knife and apply material to the wall, medium-grade sandpaper and a sanding block. The work area should be neat and dust-free.

Filling tapered-edge board joints

Start by applying a ⅛-inch-thick bed of compound to the recess around a wallboard joint with a 3-inch knife. The bed should be uniform and fairly smooth, with no voids—to accomplish this, work with firm but fluid strokes. After the bed has been prepared, lightly press wallboard tape into it with the 3-inch knife (**1**). It sometimes helps the tape to adhere if it is moistened before application. Once the tape is in position, go over it with the knife, pressing firmly and using the knife edge to smooth the tape and squeeze out excess compound from beneath it. Work in only one direction and after each stroke, scrape the knife blade against the edge of the hawk to remove excess compound. It is critical that no air bubbles are left beneath the tape, but it is equally crucial that the surface is not overworked.

Stop working the surface if the compound begins to dry.

Allow the initial coat of compound and tape to dry for about a day. Inspect the first coat for ridges, burrs and air bubbles beneath the tape. Sand lightly with a block to remove ridges; dried burrs can usually be scraped off with a clean taping knife. Cut away tape over air bubbles with a utility knife.

Apply a thinner second coat of compound over the tape using a 4- or 6-inch taping knife (**2**). Fill all voids and feather the edges of the bead. Allow the second coat to dry thoroughly and remove any surface roughness as after the first application.

The third and final coat should be applied with an 8- or 10-inch knife (**3**). When dry, the final coat may be lightly polished with medium-grade sandpaper.

CUT EDGES

Treat a butt joint between a tapered edge and a cut edge of wallboard in a way similar to that described for joints between two tapered edges (see left), but build up the tapered edge with compound, level with the cut edge, before applying the tape.

When two cut edges meet press the compound into the ⅛-inch gap to finish flush. When the compound is set, apply a thin band of finish to it and press the paper tape tight against the board. Cover this with a wide but thin coat of compound and feather the edges, then finish off as before.

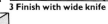

FIBERGLASS TAPES

A self-adhesive fiberglass mesh tape can be used instead of traditional paper tape for finishing new wallboard or for making patch repairs. The tape is a strong binder and does not need prior application of compound to bond it in place. The tape is put on first, then the compound is pressed through the mesh afterwards.

Applying the tape
Make sure that the joint edges of the wallboard are dust-free. If the edges of boards have been cut, burnish them with the handle of your taping knife to remove all traces of rough paper.

Starting at the top, center the tape over the joint, unroll and press it into place as your work down the wall. Cut it off to length at the bottom. Do not overlap ends if you have to make a join in the tape; butt them.

Press the compound through the tape into the joint with the knife, then level off the surface so that the mesh of the tape is visible and let the compound set.

Finish the joint with subsequent coats of compound, as with paper tape.

Applying the compound
Press the compound through the tape with a taping knife.

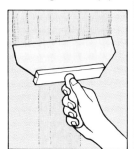

1 Press tape into filler   **2 Apply finish in a wide band**   **3 Finish with wide knife**

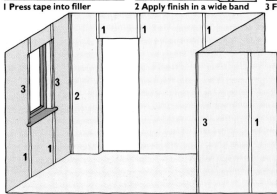

Filling the joints
1 Use the tape flat for flush joints.
2 Fold the tape for inside corners.
3 Use metal-reinforced tape or metal corner bead on outside corners.

FINISHING WALLBOARD

Inside corners

The inside corners of drywall are finished in a way similar to the method used for flat joints. A bed of joint compound is first applied to the contiguous surfaces where two walls meet to form a corner or where a wall meets the ceiling.

Cut the paper tape to length and fold it down its center. Use a 3-inch joint knife or a specially designed corner knife

to press the paper into the wet compound (1).

Squeeze out excess compound from beneath the tape and remove it. You may wish to apply the second coat of compound over the tape immediately (2). Feather the edges with a wide knife.

When the first coat is completely dry, apply a second, wider coat and feather the edges again.

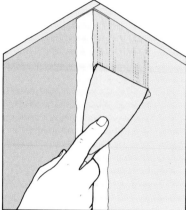

1 Finishing inside corner
Apply bands of compound to adjacent walls, creasing tape, and then pressing tape into wet compound.

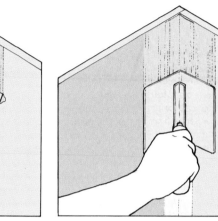

2 Applying coat of compound coat and tape
This can be done with a special corner knife. Feathering coats are applied with wider flat knives.

Outside corners

Wallboard edges that meet to form an outside corner must first have a corner bead applied over them. There are two basic designs for corner beads—one has a thin, metal rod attached to paper flanges, the other is all-metal. The paper type must be embedded in compound, and the all-metal type is fastened to the corner with drywall nails, screws or a

special crimping tool. If nails or screws are used, it is essential that the fastener heads be driven below the protruding surface of the bead, but care must be taken not to distort the metal flanges into which the fasteners are driven.

Once the corner bead has been fastened to the surface, the flanges are covered with successive applications of wallboard compound. The first coat should be applied with one edge of the knife blade resting against the bead extension and the other against the wallboard surface. The slight hollow is filled with a relatively thick coat of compound. Once the first coat is dry, scrape off the burrs with a clean joint knife and apply two more coats with successively wider knives to fill the hollow and feather out the edges of the compound.

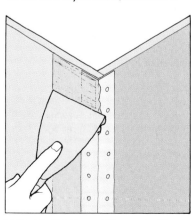

Method for finishing outside corner with corner bead and compound

PREPARING FOR DECORATION

Finishing with plaster
The alternative to direct decoration of the gypsum wallboard is to precede decoration by applying a thin finishing-coat of actual plaster to the board. The plastering is not easy for the inexperienced but with some practice, you could tackle your walls. Ceilings should be left to professionals, but you can prepare the wallboard and have it ready for the tradesman to plaster.

Preparing the ground
First fill the gaps between the board joints and at the angles, bringing them flush with the boards. Use board-finish plaster for one-coat plastering, and an undercoat first for two-coat plastering.

Reinforce all of the joints and angles with jute scrim pressed into a thin band of the plaster. Let the plaster set, but don't let it dry out before applying the finishing plaster.

Rolls of jute scrim 3½-inches-wide are available from builders' suppliers.

If you intend to plaster the walls yourself, first study the section on plastering thoroughly (▷).

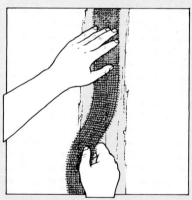

Reinforce joints with scrim before plastering

Decorating direct
Before the wallboard can be directly decorated, it must be given a uniform surface by the application of a sealer.

Brush on or sponge-apply a thin coating of finish mixed to a thin consistency. If applying it by brush, follow it up with the sponge worked in a light circular motion over the entire surface. Alternatively, use a proprietary ready-mixed top coat, which can be applied with a brush or roller and is suitable for all decorative treatments. Two coats of shellac will also provide a vapor barrier.

APPLYING GYPSUM BOARD TO A CEILING

A new ceiling may be made with wallboard, which can also be used to replace an old lath-and-plaster ceiling that is beyond repair.

Fastening wallboard in place and finishing its surface to make it ready for direct decoration can be tackled by the non-professional, but wet plastering of a ceiling should be left to the skilled professional as it is hard work and difficult to do well.

Preparing an old ceiling

Start by stripping away all the old damaged plaster and lath, and pull out all the nails.

This is a messy job, so wear protective clothing, a pair of goggles and a face mask while working. It's also a good idea to seal the gaps around doors in the room to prevent dust escaping through the rest of the house.

If necessary, trim back the top edge of the wall plaster so that the edge of the ceiling wallboard can be tucked in.

Inspect and treat exposed joists for any signs of decay.

FITTING NEW WALLBOARD

Measure the area of the ceiling and select the most economical size of boards to cover it.

The boards should be fitted with their long paper-covered edges running at right angles to the joists. The butting joints between the ends of boards should be staggered on each row and supported by a joist in every case.

Fit perimeter nailers between the joists against the walls and other intermediate ones in lines across the ceilings to support the long edges of the boards. It is not always necessary to fit intermediate supports if the boards are finally to be plastered, but they will guarantee a sound ceiling. The intermediate nailers should be 2-by-4 and should be fitted so that the edges of the boards will fall along their center lines.

If necessary, trim the length of the boards to guarantee that their ends fall on the center lines of the joists.

Start applying the boards working from one corner of the room. It takes two people to support a large sheet of wallboard while it is being fastened. Smaller sizes may be applied single-handed, but even then a temporary wooden prop to hold them in place during nailing will be useful.

Using galvanized wallboard nails, install the first board, working from the joist nearest its center and nailing at 6-inch centers. This is to prevent the boards sagging in the middle, which can happen if their edges are nailed first.

Fasten all the remaining boards in the same way.

If the boards are to be plastered, leave ⅛-inch gaps between the cut ends and the paper-covered edges. For direct decoration, butt the paper-covered edges but leave ⅛-inch gaps at the ends of the boards.

Finish the joints by the method described for gypsum wallboard (◁).

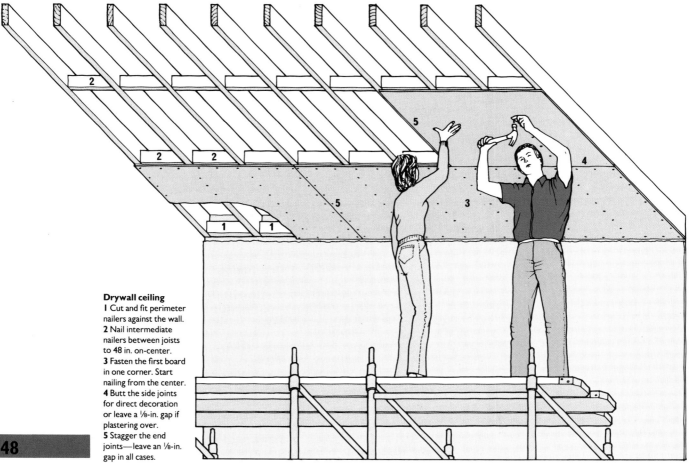

Drywall ceiling
1 Cut and fit perimeter nailers against the wall.
2 Nail intermediate nailers between joists to 48 in. on-center.
3 Fasten the first board in one corner. Start nailing from the center.
4 Butt the side joints for direct decoration or leave a ⅛-in. gap if plastering over.
5 Stagger the end joints—leave an ⅛-in. gap in all cases.

Taping the joint

Where new gypsum wallboard panels meet a ceiling, the joint must be taped and successive coats of compound applied as for any inside corner in gypsum wallboard construction. This is the case whether the ceiling has been also finished with wallboard or it is an existing plaster ceiling.

As you would with an inside corner formed by two walls, apply a thick coat of compound to the adjacent surfaces with a 3-in. joint knife or corner taping knife. Fold the tape lengthwise and press it into the wet compound. Then use the flat or corner knife to smooth the tape and remove excess compound and air bubbles. Let the freshly applied compound dry for about 24 hours, polish and smooth the dry compound as necessary, then apply a second coat of compound to both the wall and ceiling surfaces with a 6-inch knife, feathering the edges flush with the wall and ceiling surfaces. After the second coat dries, prepare the surface and then apply the final coat of compound with an 8- to 10-inch knife. Once the final coat is dry and after it has had minor imperfections either filled or polished out with sandpaper, the walls and ceiling will be ready for decorating.

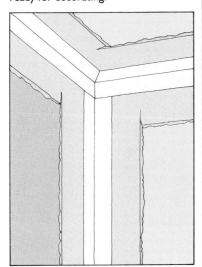

Finishing joints between wallboard and ceiling
Use compound and a folded length of tape, then feather out as ordinary joints.

Crown moldings

Millwork designed to finish the corner formed by a ceiling and the top of a wall is called "crown molding." There are many sizes, patterns and profiles of crown molding, and at least several choices are likely to be available at your local lumberyard or home center. A great number of patterns are also available in molded polystyrene plastic and are available through lumberyards, decorator outlets and by mail order.

Whether you choose a wide, highly detailed style or a simple design, treating walls with crown moldings can provide an extremely nice decorative touch. Of course, the crown molding you select should be in keeping with other trim moldings used in the room and its overall style.

As with other moldings whose ends must be miter-cut to form corners, it is necessary to use a miter box when cutting crown molding. But, because crown moldings are applied between the wall and ceiling at a cant, the ends must take a compound, rather than simple, miter-cut. It is easy to cut compound miters accurately if the crown molding is supported in the miter box at the same angle at which it will be applied to the wall. One method of supporting the molding would be to construct a jig from two pieces of wood joined along their edges to form a right angle, as shown at the right. The widths of the pieces used to make the jig must

be such that the crown molding can be nestled into them to form the hypotenuse of a right triangle. It is also helpful to cut the ends of the top part of the jig to parallel 45-degree angles.

After determining the length needed for a particular run of crown molding, mark the point at which it must be cut along the top of the molding. Nestle the molding into the jig and align the cutting mark with the 45-degree miter box guides. Hold the molding and jig tightly against the back of the miter box and cut on the waste side of the mark with a sharp backsaw. It is important to establish the correct direction of the cut—if the miter is being cut for an inside corner, the back of the cut piece will, in effect, be longer than the patterned face. The opposite will be the case for crown moldings cut to form an outside corner.

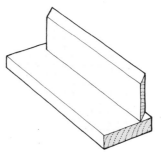

Jig for cutting compound miters for crown molding with a miter box and backsaw

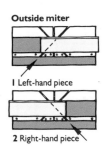

Outside miter

1 Left-hand piece

2 Right-hand piece

Inside miter

1 Left-hand piece

2 Right-hand piece

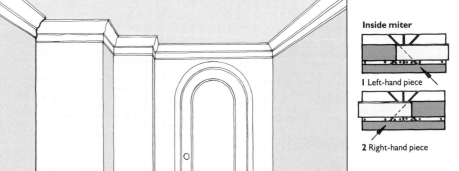

Crown molding can be used for an elegant treatment for the joint between wall and ceiling

FLOORING

Flooring is the general term used to describe the surface which is laid over the floor's structural elements—the floor joists or the concrete slab. This surface can consist of hardwood planks or strips, or it can be constructed with manufactured boards of plywood or particleboard. Resilient vinyl flooring is another option.

Floorboards

Hardwoods are generally used for making floorboards. The standard widths are from 1 to 3½ inches and thicknesses range from 5/16 to 2 inches. The standard thickness for tongue-and-groove flooring is 25/32 inch. The most popular width is 2¼ inches.

The narrow boards produce superior floors because they make any movement due to shrinkage less noticeable. But installing them is costly in labor, and they are used only in expensive houses. Softwood flooring of pine or hemlock is common in older homes, but seldom installed today.

The best floorboards are quarter-sawn (1) from the log, a method that diminishes distortion from shrinkage. But as this method is wasteful of timber, boards are more often cut tangentially (2) for reasons of economy. Boards cut in this way tend to bow, or "cup" across their width and they should be fastened with the cupped side facing upwards, as there is a tendency for the grain of the other side to splinter. The cut of a board—tangential or quarter-cut—can be checked by looking at the annual growth rings on the end grain.

The joint of tongue-and-groove boards is not at the center of their edges but closer to one face, and these boards should be laid with the offset joint nearer to the joist. Though tongue-and-groove boards are nominally the same sizes as square-edged boards, the edge joint reduces their floor coverage by about ½ inch per board.

In some old buildings, you may find floorboards bearing the marks left by an adze on their undersides. Such old boards have usually been trimmed to a required thickness only where they sit over the joists, while their top faces and edges are planed smooth.

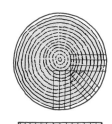

1 Quarter-sawn boards
Shrinkage does not distort these boards.

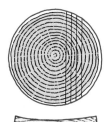

2 Tangentially sawn boards
Shrinkage can cause these boards to "cup"

SHEET FLOORING

Softwood and hardwood boards not only provide a tough flooring, but when sealed and polished they will also take on an attractive color. But sheet materials such as flooring-grade plywood or particleboard are purely functional, and are only as subfloor surfaces.

Plywood
Plywood is the most commonly used subfloor material. Standard thickness is 3/8 or 3/4 inch; sheets are normally 4 × 8 feet. Special 1 1/8-inch plywood milled with tongue-and-groove edges is sometimes used to provide underlayment for carpeting. (Normally, underlayment is added as a separate layer.) Subfloor-grade plywood has one smooth side and one rough. Many grades are available. Most codes allow B-C, C-C, and C-D.

Particleboard
Particleboard for subflooring is allowed by some building codes. It is less expensive than plywood. Though particleboard does not warp, it does absorb moisture. Sheets come in 2 × 8- and 4 × 8-foot sizes, and for subfloor use, thicknesses of 3/8 to 3/4 inch. Both square-edged and tongue-and-groove panels are available. Particleboard is harder to nail into than plywood, and dulls sawblades faster. However, where the material is liable to become slightly damp only occasionally, some builders prefer it to plywood because it won't delaminate.

Types of flooring
1 Square-edged particleboard
2 T&G particleboard
3 T&G plywood
4 T&G softwood boards
5 Square-edged softwood boards
6 T&G hardwood boards

TONGUE-AND-GROOVE FLOORING

You can detect whether your floorboards are tongue-and-groove by trying to push a knife blade into the gap between them.

To lift a tongue-and-groove board it is necessary first to cut through the tongues on each side of the board. Saw carefully along the line of the joint with a dovetail or tenon saw (**1**) held at a shallow angle. A straight strip temporarily nailed along the edge of the board may help you to keep the saw on a straight line.

With the tongue cut through, saw across the board and lift it as you would a square-edged one.

If the original flooring has been "blind nailed" (**2**), use finishing nails (**3**) to nail the boards back in place and conceal the recesses with a matching wood filler.

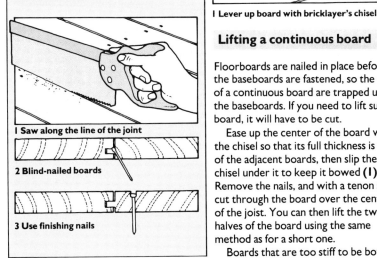

1 Saw along the line of the joint

2 Blind-nailed boards

3 Use finishing nails

REFITTING A CUT BOARD

The butted ends of floorboards normally meet and rest on a joist (**1**) and a board which has been cut flush with the side of a joist must be given a new means of support when replaced (**2**).

Cut a piece of 2 × 2-in. softwood and screw it to the side of the joists flush with the top. Screw the end of the floorboard to the support.

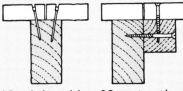

1 Boards share a joist   **2 Support a cut board**

LIFTING FLOORBOARDS

Floorboards are produced in random lengths which are an equal size per bundle—oak strips are often up to 16 feet long. When lifting floorboards, it is these shorter pieces that you should start with if possible. In many older homes, one or two boards will probably have been lifted already for access to services.

Square-edged boards

Tap the blade of a bricklayer's chisel (▷) into the gap between the boards close to the cut end (**1**). Lever up the edge of the board but try not to crush the edge of the one next to it. Fit the prybar into the gap at the other side of the board and repeat the procedure.

Ease the end of the board up in this way, then work the claw of a hammer under it until you can lift it enough to slip a cold chisel (▷) under it (**2**). Move along the board to the next set of nails and proceed in the same way, continuing until the board comes away.

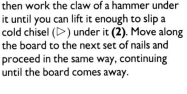

1 Lever up board with bricklayer's chisel   **2 Place cold chisel under board**

Lifting a continuous board

Floorboards are nailed in place before the baseboards are fastened, so the ends of a continuous board are trapped under the baseboards. If you need to lift such a board, it will have to be cut.

Ease up the center of the board with the chisel so that its full thickness is clear of the adjacent boards, then slip the cold chisel under it to keep it bowed (**1**). Remove the nails, and with a tenon saw cut through the board over the center of the joist. You can then lift the two halves of the board using the same method as for a short one.

Boards that are too stiff to be bowed upwards, or are tongue-and-groove, will have to be cut across in place. This means cutting flush with the side of the joist instead of over its center.

Locate the side of the joist by passing the blade of a padsaw (**2**) vertically into the gaps on both sides of the board (the joints of tongue-and-groove boards will also have to be cut (see left). Mark the edges of the board where the blade stops, and draw a line between these points representing the side of the joist. Make a starting hole for the saw blade by drilling three or four ⅛-inch holes close together at one end of the line marked across the surface.

Work the tip of the blade into the hole and start making the cut with short strokes. Gradually tip the blade to a shallow angle to avoid cutting into any cables or pipes that may be hidden below. Lever up the board with a chisel as described above.

Freeing the end of a board

The end of the board trapped under the baseboard can usually be freed by being lifted to a steep angle, when the gap between the joists and the wall should allow the board to clear the nails and be pulled free (**1**).

To raise a floorboard that runs beneath a partition wall, the board must also be cut close to the wall. Drill a starting hole and then cut the board as close to the wall as possible (**2**).

There is a special saw (**3**) that can be used for cutting floorboards. It has a curved cutting edge that allows you to cut a board without fully lifting it.

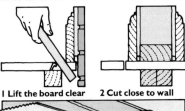

1 Lift the board clear   **2 Cut close to wall**

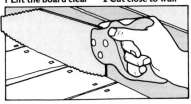

3 Use a floorboard saw if necessary

SEE ALSO

Details for:▷
| Bricklayer's chisel | 77 |
| Cold chisel | 77 |

1 Saw across the board

2 Find the joist's side

RE-LAYING A FLOOR

Though floors probably take more wear and tear than any other interior surface, this is not usually the reason why re-laying boards becomes necessary. Fire damage or wood decay—which would also affect the joists—or simply large gaps in the boards caused by shrinkage may require the floor to be relaid, or even entirely renewed.

If the floor is to be renewed, measure the room and buy your materials in advance. Leave floorboards or sheets of plywood to acclimatize—ideally in the room where they are to be laid—for at least a week before fastening them.

Removing the flooring

To lift the complete flooring you must first remove the baseboards from the walls (◁). If you intend to re-lay the boards, number them with chalk before starting to raise them. Lift the first few boards as described (◁), starting from one side of the room, then pry up the remainder by working a cold chisel or crowbar between the joists and the undersides of the boards. In the case of tongue-and-groove boards, two or three should be eased up simultaneously, to avoid breaking the joints, and progressively pulled away.

Pull all the nails out of the boards and joists, and scrape any accumulated dirt from the tops of the joists. Clean the edges of the boards similarly if they are to be reused. Check all boards for rot or insect infestation and treat or repair them as required.

Laying new floorboards

Though the following deals with fixing tongue-and-groove floorboards, the basic method described applies equally to square-edged boards.

Lay a few loose boards together to form a work platform. Measure the width or length of the room —whichever is at right angles to the joists— and cut your boards to stop ⅜ inch short of the walls at each end. Where two shorter boards are to be butted end to end, cut them so that the joint will be centered on a joist and set the boards out so as to avoid such joints occurring on the same joist with adjacent boards. Any two butt joints must be separated by at least one whole board. Lay four to six boards at a time.

Fix the first board with its grooved edge no more than ⅜ inch from the wall and nail it in place with steel-cuts—or finishing nails that are at least twice as long as the thickness of the board.

Place the nails in pairs, one about 1 inch from each edge of the board and centered on the joists. Punch them in about 1/16 inch. Place one nail in the tongued edge if blind-nailing.

Lay the other cut boards in place and clamp them to the fixed one so as to close the edge joints. Special floorboard clamps can be rented for this, but wedges cut from 16-inch cut-offs of board will work just as well (**1**). To clamp the boards with wedges, temporarily nail another board just less than a board's width away from them. Insert the pairs of wedges in the gap, resting on every fourth or fifth joist, and with two hammers tap the wedges' wide ends toward each other. Nail the clamped-up boards in place as before, then remove the wedges and temporary board and repeat the operation with the next group of boards, continuing in this way across the room.

At the far wall, place the remaining boards, cutting the last one to width, its tongue on the "waste" side. It should be cut to leave a gap equal to the width of the tongue or ½ inch, whichever is less. If you cannot get the last board to slot in, cut away the bottom section of the grooved edge so that it will drop into place (**2**).

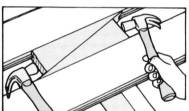

1 Make wedges to clamp boards

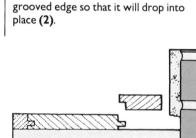

2 Cut away part of last board's grooved edge

- **Closing gaps**
You can re-lay floorboards without removing all the boards at once. Lift and renail about six boards at a time as you work across the floor. Finally, cut and fit a new board to fill the last gap.

Laying the boards
Working from a platform of loose boards, proceed in the following order:
1 Nail first board parallel to the wall.
2 Cut and lay up to six boards, clamp them together and nail.
3 Lay the next group of boards in the same way, continue across the floor and cut the last board to fit.

FLOORBOARD CLAMP

This special tool automatically grips the joist over which it is placed by means of two toothed cams. A screw-operated ram applies pressure to the floorboards when the bar is turned.

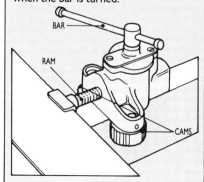

LAYING PARTICLEBOARD FLOORING

For a floor that is going to be invisible beneath some kind of covering—whether vinyl, cork, fitted carpet or whatever—particleboard is an excellent material. It is laid relatively quickly and is much cheaper than an equivalent amount of hardwood flooring. It comes in two types—square-edged or tongue-and-groove. Each has its own laying technique.

CUTTING TO FIT

Square-edge boards
The widths of the boards may have to be cut down (1) so that their long edges will butt on the joists' center lines.

Tongue-and-groove boards
Only the last boards need be cut in their width (2) to fit against the wall.

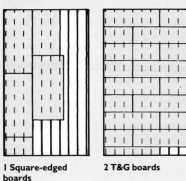

1 Square-edged boards **2 T&G boards**

Square-edged boards

All the edges of a square-edged chipboard flooring must be supported. Lay the boards with their long edges along the joists and nail 2 × 4 blocking between the joists to support the boards' ends. The blocking against the wall can be placed in advance; those supporting joints must be nailed into place as the boards are laid.

Start with a full-length board in one corner and lay a row of boards the length of the room, cutting the last one to fit as required. Leave an expansion gap of about 3/8 inch between the outer edges of the boards and the walls. If the boards' inner edges do not fall on the center line of a joist, cut them down so that they do so on the nearest one, but cut the surplus off the outer edge, near the wall.

Nail the boards down close together, using 2- or 2¼-inch annular ring nails spaced about 1 foot apart along the joists and blocking. Place the nails about ¾ inch from the edges. Cut and lay the remainder of the boards with the end joints staggered on alternate rows.

Tongue-and-groove boards

Tongue-and-groove boards are laid with their long edges running across the joists. Blocking is needed only against the walls, to support the outer edges. The ends of the boards are supported by joists.

Working from one corner, lay the first board with its grooved edges about 3/8 inch from the walls and nail it into place.

Apply PVA wood adhesive to the joint along the end of the first board, then lay the next one in the row. Knock it up to the first board with a hammer for a good close joint, protecting the edge with a piece of scrap wood. Nail the board down as before, then wipe any surplus adhesive from the surface before it sets, using a damp rag. Continue in this way across the floor, gluing all of the joints as you go. Cut boards to fit at the ends of rows or to fall on the center of a joist, and stagger these end joints on alternate rows. Finally, fit the baseboard, which will cover the expansion gaps.

You can seal the surface of the particleboard with two coats of clear polyurethane if you wish, to protect it from dirt.

1 Square-edged boards
Lay the boards with their long edges on a joist and the ends supported with blocking.

2 Tongue-and-groove boards
Lay the boards across the joists with the ends falling on a joist.

1 Arrangement for laying square-edged boards

2 Arrangement for laying T&G boards

FLOOR JOISTS

Floor joists are important structural elements of a house. Being loadbearing, their size and spacing in new structures are strictly specified by building code regulations and they must satisfy a building inspector. Spacing and lumber dimension are the most critical factors. In most cases, repairing and replacing joists may be done merely using the same size lumber as the originals. However, it is always recommended that you consult building regulations or a building inspector before beginning any task involving joists, especially in the case of older homes.

Fitting services

Service runs like heating pipes and electric cables can run in the void below a suspended first floor, but those running at right angles to the joists in upper floors must pass through the joists, which are covered by flooring above and a ceiling below.

So as not to weaken joists, the holes for cables and pipes should center on the joists depth, in any event at least 2 inches below the top surface to clear floor nails, and always within the middle two-thirds of the joist's length (1).

Notches for pipe runs in the top edge should be no deeper than one-fourth the depth of the joist and within a quarter of the joist's length at each end. Otherwise, they will be weakened. Notched joists should be strengthened along their length with 2 × 4s (2). Make notches by drilling through the joist, then sawing down to the hole.

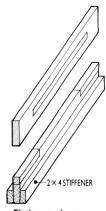

— 2 X 4 STIFFENER

Fitting services
1 Make holes within the shaded line.
2 Place notches within shaded area.

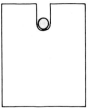

Drill and saw notches to accommodate pipe

Repairing joists

Repairing joists is far simpler than replacing them. To fit new joists, long lengths must often be maneuvered where there is little headroom, and frequently fitting new joists causes uneven spots in an otherwise level floor.

If possible, repair joists by strengthening localized areas of damage, using either metal fittings such as joist hangers and angle iron, steel plates or ¾-inch plywood strips. Weak and sagging joists can be strengthened by attaching a long length of angle iron along their bottom edge, or by fastening them to new joists, running parallel.

Sometimes deteriorated wood can be treated with insecticide to prevent further damage, and new wood placed on either side, separated from the infected wood by a layer of 15-pound asphalt roofing felt placed in between. Check with an exterminator. However, in most cases of rot or insect damage, new wood is the only answer. Again, where code allows, you may be able merely to cut out the decayed wood and replace it with a new section properly strengthened. Where regulations require that new wood stretch from sill to sill or sill to girder, however, you will have to install full-length lumber.

Fitting a new joist

To replace joists resting atop sills, first notch the ends as shown. Position the joist on its side, next to the old joist, then tap it snugly into place on edge using a light sledgehammer. Stop and trim the upper edge of the joist if the floor shows signs of lifting. After the new joist is in place, jack both joists up slightly and insert thin shims against the notched surface. Lower the jacks, then nail the joists together using 16d common nails.

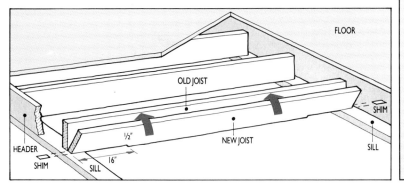

FLOOR
OLD JOIST
SHIM
½"
NEW JOIST
SILL
HEADER
SHIM
SILL
16"

STRENGTHENING A SAGGING FLOOR

When sections of flooring become uneven, usually a problem in older homes, the cause is seldom the joists but more often the weakening of a girder or supporting post. One remedy is to merely add another post, directly beneath the sagging section of girder. Rent a shoring jack and use it to raise the girder to level, plus a fraction of an inch more to allow for settling. Raise the jack very gradually, a partial turn or so per day over the course of a week or more. Adjust the height of the new post and make sure there is solid footing beneath (a 20-inch-square concrete slab 10 inches thick is standard). Then fit the post into position, check that it is exactly vertical, and lower the girder onto it as you remove the jack. Sometimes all that is necessary is to place shims between the girder and existing posts, using the same jacking method.

To determine the amount a girder must be raised to level it, stretch a string along one side of the beam, from the bottom corner at one end to the bottom corner at the other. The amount of wood showing below the string (where the sag is most extreme) is the distance the girder must be raised.

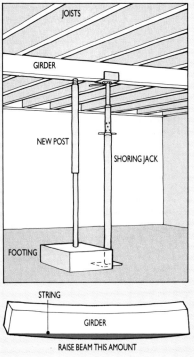

JOISTS
GIRDER
NEW POST
SHORING JACK
FOOTING
STRING
GIRDER
RAISE BEAM THIS AMOUNT

BASEBOARDS

Baseboards are protective "kick boards," but are usually also molded to form a decorative border between the floor and walls. Modern baseboards are relatively small and simply formed, with either a rounded or beveled top edge.

Baseboards found in older houses can be as much as 1 foot wide and quite elaborately molded, but those in newer homes are narrower and simpler. Many designs are available at lumberyards. Some will supply more elaborate designs to special order.

Baseboards can be nailed directly onto studs behind wallboard. Sometimes a strip of quarter-round molding is attached also, where the baseboard meets the floor.

BASEBOARD MOLDINGS

Most standard baseboard moldings are made in softwood ready for painting. Hardwood is not so common and is reserved for special decorative boards. Hardwoods are coated with a clear finish. "Molded-reverse" baseboards have a different profile machined on each side of the board—providing two boards in one.

Removing baseboard molding

Remove a baseboard by levering it away from the wall with a crowbar or bricklayer's chisel. Where a baseboard butts against door molding or an outside corner, it can be levered off, but a single length whose ends are mitered into inside corners will have to be cut before it can be removed.

Tap the blade of the chisel between the baseboard and the wall, and lever the top edge away sufficiently to insert the chisel end of the crowbar behind it. Place a thin strip of wood behind the crowbar to protect the wall, tap the chisel in again a little further, and work along the baseboard in this way as the nails loosen. With the board removed, pull the nails out through the back to avoid splitting the face. If you're careful, you can reuse the molding.

Cutting a long baseboard

A long stretch of baseboard will bend out sufficiently for you to cut it in place if you lever it away at its center and insert blocks of wood (**1**), one on each side of the proposed cut, to hold the board about 1 inch from the wall.

Make a vertical cut with a panel saw held at about 45 degrees to the face of the board (**2**) and work with short strokes, using the tip of the saw.

Selection of baseboard moldings
(From top to bottom) Beveled hardwoods. Beveled/rounded reverse. Ovolo/beveled reverse. Torus/beveled reverse. Ovolo/torus reverse. Hardwood baseboard.

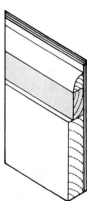

Making a baseboard
If you are unable to buy a length of baseboard to match your original, and the cost of having it specially machined is too high, make it up from various sections of molding.

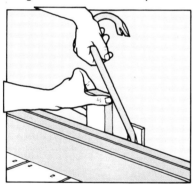

1 Pry board away from wall and shim it out

2 Cut through baseboard with tip of saw

Fitting new baseboard

A baseboard can be damaged by excessive moisture or dryness, or it can suffer in the process of being removed when a repair to a floor is being made. Restore the board if you can, especially if it is a special molding; otherwise try to make it up from various molded sections (see right). Standard moldings are easily available through lumberyards.

Measure the length of the wall. Most baseboards are mitered at the corners, so take this into account when you are measuring between inside and outside corners.

Mark the length on the plain bottom edge of the board, then mark a 45-degree angle on the edge and square it across the face of the board. Fix the board on edge in a vise and carefully cut down the line at that angle.

Sometimes molded baseboards are scribed and butt-jointed at inside corners. To achieve the profile, cut the end off one board at 45 degrees as you would for a miter joint (**1**), and with a coping saw cut along the contour line on the molded face so that it will "jig-saw" with its neighbor (**2**).

Fasten baseboards with cut nails when nailing to brickwork and with finishing nails when attaching them to wood wall framing.

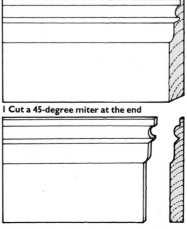

1 Cut a 45-degree miter at the end

2 Cut the shape following the contour line

DOORS: TYPES AND CONSTRUCTION

At first glance there appears to be a great variety of doors to choose from, but in fact most of the differences are simply stylistic. All doors are all based on a small number of construction methods.

The wide range of styles can sometimes tempt homeowners into buying doors that are inappropriate to the houses they live in. When replacing a front door you should be careful to choose one that is not incongruous with the architectural style of your house.

Buying a door

Doors in softwood and hardwood are available, the latter being the more expensive and normally used for a special interior or an entrance where the natural features of the wood can be exploited to the best effect.

Softwood doors are for more general use and are intended to be painted as opposed to clear-finished.

Glazed doors are becoming common features in the front and rear entrances of today's houses. They are traditionally of wooden frame construction, though modern aluminium-framed doors can be bought in the standard sizes, complete with double-glazing and accessories.

Wood-framed and panel doors are supplied in unfinished wood; these require trimming, glazing and fitting out with hinges, locks and letter plates.

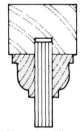

Exterior flush door
A central rail is fitted to take a letter plate.

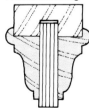

1 Planted molding

2 Bolection molding

DOOR SIZES

Doors are made in several standard sizes to meet most domestic needs.

The range of heights is usually 6 feet 6 inches, 6 feet 8 inches and occasionally 7 feet. The widths range from 2 feet to 3 feet in increments of 2 inches. Thicknesses vary from 1 3/8 to 1 3/4 inches.

In older houses it is common to find that larger doors have been used for the main room on the first floor than for others, but modern homes tend to have standard-size joinery and all interior doors the same size. The standard is usually 6 feet 8 inches × 2 feet 6 inches, though front entrance doors are always larger than interior ones to suit the proportions of the building.

When replacing doors in an old house, where the openings may well be nonstandard sizes, buy one of the nearest size and cut it down, removing an equal amount from each edge to preserve the frame's symmetry.

Panel doors

Panel doors are more attractive than flush doors but are also more expensive. They have hardwood or softwood frames, mortise-and-tenon joints, with grooves that house the panels, which can be of solid wood, plywood or glass.

1 Muntins
These are the central vertical members of the door. They are jointed into the three cross rails.

2 Panels
These may be of solid wood or of plywood. They are held loosely in grooves in the frame to allow for shrinkage without splitting. They stiffen the door.

3 Cross rails
Top, center and bottom rails are tenoned into the stiles. In cheaper doors the mortise-and-tenon joints are replaced with dowel joints.

4 Stiles
These are the upright members at the sides of the door. They carry the hinges and door locks.

Panel door moldings
The frame's inner edges may be plain or molded as a decorative border. Small moldings can be machined on the frame before assembly or pinned to the inside edge. Ordinary planted molding (**1**) can shrink from the frame, making cracks in the paintwork. Bolection molding (**2**) laps the frame to overcome this. It is decorative but more vulnerable.

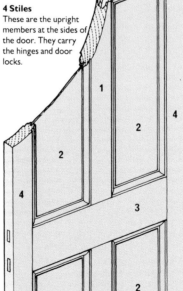

Panel door

Flush doors

Flush doors are softwood frames with plywood or hardboard covering both sides and packed with a core material. Used mainly internally, they are lightweight, cheap, simple and rather lacking in character. Exterior flush doors have a central rail to take a letter plate. Firecheck doors are a special fire-retardant grade.

1 Top and bottom rails
These are tenoned into the stiles (side pieces).

2 Intermediate rails
These lighter rails, jointed to the stiles, are notched to allow passage of air and prevent the panels from sinking.

3 Lock blocks
A softwood block to take a mortise lock is glued to each stile.

4 Panels
The plywood or hardboard panels are left plain for painting or finished with a wood veneer. Metal-skinned doors may be had to special order.

Core material
Paper or cardboard honeycomb is sometimes sandwiched between the panels. In firecheck doors, a fire-retardant material is used.

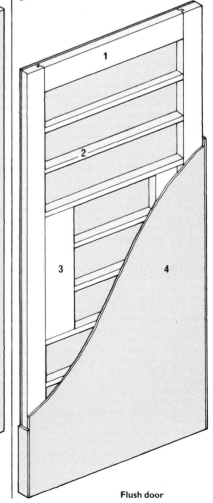

Flush door

DOORS: TYPES AND CONSTRUCTION

Ledged and braced doors

These doors have a rustic, cottagey look and are often found in old houses, outbuildings and garden walls. They are weather-resistant, strong, secure and cheap, but a little crude. A superior framed version is tenon-jointed instead of being merely nailed.

1 Battens
Tongue-and-groove boards are nailed to the ledges.

2 Strap-hinges
Butt hinges will not hold in the end-grain of the ledges, so long strap-hinges take the weight.

3 Braces
These diagonals, notched into the ledges, transmit the weight to the hinges and stop the door from sagging.

4 Ledges
These are the cross rails to which the battens are nailed.

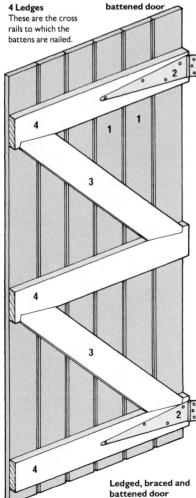

Framed, ledged, braced and battened door

Ledged, braced and battened door

DOOR FRAMES

Exterior doors

An exterior door is fitted into a heavy wooden frame consisting of the head jamb (1) at the top, the sill (2) below, fitted with a threshold and weatherstrip (inset), and the side jambs (3), which are usually joined to the other pieces by dado joints.

Normally, a section of the floor framing must be notched to accept the sill. However, some prehung exterior doors are made with adjustable sills which require no cutting. Thresholds come in several styles. They are designed to seal the door at the bottom, yet allow the door to swing freely.

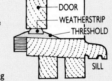

Exterior door frame
1 Head jamb
2 Sill
3 Side jamb
4 Doorstop rabbet
5 Notched floor framing

Interior doors

Interior doors are hung in frames similar to those for exterior doors, but less sturdy. No sill is present, although in some cases a threshold may be added. Usually, interior doors are trimmed during installation to leave a small amount of space above the top of the finish flooring.

The head jamb (1) and side jambs (2) are fastened to the framed rough opening with shims (3, 4) sandwiched between to level and plumb the frame, and to space it evenly within the opening. Wedge-shaped sections of cedar shingles make excellent shims. They are fastened in place with finishing nails driven through the jamb and into the pieces of the rough frame.

Interior door frame
1 Head jamb
2 Side jamb
3 Side shims
4 Head shims

Most interior doors come prehung, already mounted in frames. When selecting interior doors, make sure the jamb width is sized to fit the thickness of the wall in which it will be installed, or else choose a doorframe with adjustable-width jambs, available from some manufacturers.

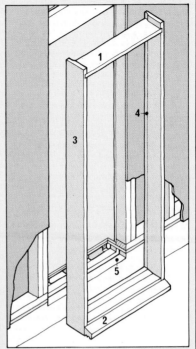

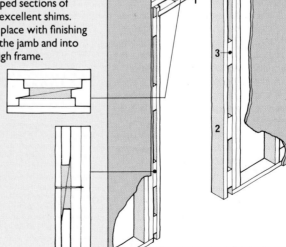

SEE ALSO

Details for: ▷

Hanging doors	58
Thresholds	59
Pre-hung doors	60
Replacing rotted frames	61

FITTING AND HANGING DOORS

Whatever the style of door you wish to fit, the procedure is the same, though minor differences between some exterior doors may show themselves. Two good-quality 4-inch butt hinges are enough to support a standard door, but if you are hanging a heavy hardwood door, you should add a third, central hinge.

All doors are fairly heavy, and as it is necessary to try a door in its frame several times to get the fit right, you will find that the job goes much more quickly and easily if you have a helper working with you.

Fitting a door

Before attaching the hinges to a new door, make sure that it fits nicely into its frame. It should have a clearance of ¹/₁₆ inch at the top and sides and should clear the floor by at least ¼ inch. As much as ½ inch may be required for a carpeted floor.

Measure the height and width of the door opening and the depth of the rabbet in the door frame into which the door must fit. Choose a door of the right thickness and, if you cannot get one that will fit the opening exactly, one which is large enough to be cut down.

Cutting to size
Transfer the measurements from the frame to the door, making necessary allowance for the clearances all around. To reduce the width of the door, stand it on edge with its latch stile upwards while it is steadied in a portable vise. Plane the stile down to the marked line, working only on the one side if a small amount is to be taken off. If a lot is to be removed, take some off each side. This is especially important with panel doors to preserve the symmetry.

If you need to take off more than ¼ inch to reduce the height of the door, remove it with a saw and finish off with a plane. Otherwise, plane the waste off (**1**). The plane must be sharp to deal with the end grain of the stiles. Work from each corner towards the center to avoid "chipping out" the corners. If you must trim a panel door by more than 4 inches, remove the waste entirely from the bottom. Then refit the spline in the exposed channel.

Try the door in the frame, supporting it on shallow wedges (**2**). If it still doesn't fit, take it down and remove more wood where appropriate.

Plane to size

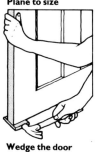
Wedge the door

Fitting hinges

The upper hinge is set about 7 inches from the door's top edge and the lower one about 10 inches from the bottom. They are cut equally into the stile and door frame. Wedge the door in its opening and, with the wedges tapped in to raise it to the right floor clearance, mark the positions of the hinges on both the door and frame.

Stand the door on edge, the hinge stile uppermost, open a hinge and, with its knuckle projecting from the edge of the door, align it with the marks and draw around the flap with a pencil (**1**). Set a marking gauge to the thickness of the mortise. Chisel out a series of shallow cuts across the grain (**2**) and pare out the waste to the scored line. Repeat the procedure with the second hinge, then, using the flaps as guides, drill pilot holes for the screws and fix both hinges into their mortises.

Wedge the door in the open position, aligning the free hinge flaps with the marks on the door frame. Make sure that the knuckles of the hinges are parallel with the frame, then trace the mortises on the frame (**3**) and cut them out as you did the others.

Adjusting and aligning
Hang the door with one screw holding each hinge and see if it closes smoothly. If the latch stile rubs on the frame, you may have to make one or both mortises slightly deeper. If the door strains against the hinges, it is what is called "hinge bound." In this case, insert thin cardboard strips beneath the hinge flaps to shim them out and retest door operation. When the door finally opens and closes properly, drive in the rest of the screws.

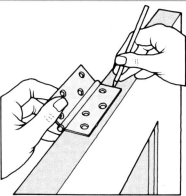
1 Mark around the flap with a pencil

2 Cut across the grain with a chisel

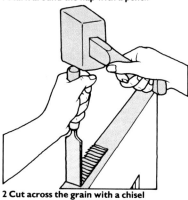
3 Mark the size of the flap on the frame

MEASUREMENTS

A door that fits well will open and close freely and look symmetrical in the frame. Use the figures given as a guide for trimming the door and setting out the position of the hinges.

⅛-in. clearance at top and sides •
Upper hinge 7 in. from the top •

Lower hinge 10 in. from the bottom •
¼- to ½-in. gap at the bottom •

Rising butt hinges

Rising butt hinges lift a door as it is opened and are fitted to prevent it from dragging on thick pile carpet.

They are made in two parts: a flap, with a fixed pin, which is screwed to the door frame, and another, with a single knuckle, which is fixed to the door, the knuckle sliding over the pin.

Rising butt hinges can be fastened only one way up, and are therefore made specifically for left- or right-hand opening. The countersunk screwholes in the fixed-pin flap indicate the side to which it is made to be fitted.

Fitting

Trim the door and mark the hinge positions (see opposite), but before fitting the hinges, plane a shallow bevel at the top outer corner of the hinge stile so that it will clear the frame as it opens. As the stile (▷) runs through to the top of the door, plane from the outer corner towards the center to avoid splitting the wood. The top strip of the door stop will mask the bevel when the door is closed.

Fit the hinges to the door and the frame, then lower the door onto the hinge pins, taking care not to damage the molding above the opening.

ADJUSTING BUTT HINGES

Perhaps you have a door catching on a bump in the floor as it opens. You can, of course, fit rising butt hinges, but the problem can be overcome by resetting the lower hinge so that its knuckle projects slightly more than the top one. The door will still hang vertically when closed, but as it opens the out-of-line pins will throw it upwards so that the bottom edge will clear the bump.

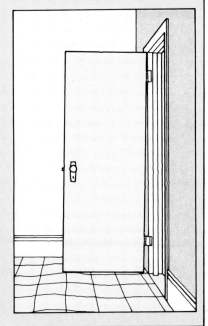

Resetting the hinge
You may have to reset both hinges to the new angle to prevent binding.

SEE ALSO

Details for: ▷
Door construction 56

Weatherstripping a door

Weatherstripping is special molding fitted to the bottom of an exterior door to prevent moisture and the flow of air underneath. Many styles are available. Some require that the door be trimmed, some do not. Often, weatherstripping comes as an integral part of the threshold itself, and is easily installed merely by screwing the threshold to the sill.

When installing a new door, consider attaching a type of weatherstrip which mounts to the bottom of the door or to the threshold directly beneath it. When retrofitting weatherstripping, a style that attaches to the inside of the door at its lower edge is easier to apply, and adjustable as well.

Weatherstripping that flexes or is walked on will wear out in time. It is a good idea to check its condition each year and replace it if necessary. The best time to do this is *before* the onset of inclement weather.

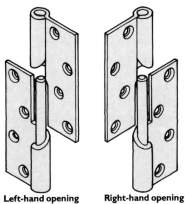

Left-hand opening   **Right-hand opening**

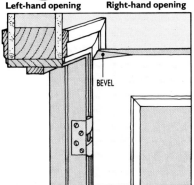

BEVEL

Plane a shallow bevel to clear the door frame

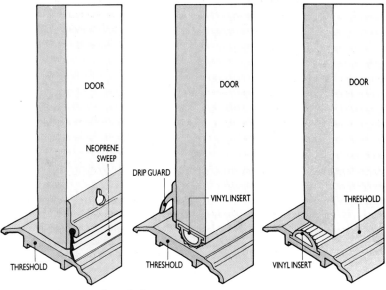

DOOR

NEOPRENE SWEEP

THRESHOLD

DOOR

DRIP GUARD

VINYL INSERT

THRESHOLD

DOOR

THRESHOLD

VINYL INSERT

Three types of door weatherstripping

INSTALLING A PRE-HUNG DOOR

Purchasing a door already attached to a matching frame saves a great deal of time and permits even novice DIYers to accomplish accurate work. Install the side of the door frame to which the door is attached first, by inserting it in the rough opening (**1**), wedged from below to allow clearance above finish flooring. Trim the lower ends of the jamb sides if necessary (**2**), then center the frame within the opening and align it horizontally and vertically using a level and plumb bob. Anchor the frame in place by shimming out the sides and head jamb with shims (**3**). Use finishing nails to fasten the shims securely to the frame and rough opening. Also drive finishing nails through the door casing into the edges of the rough opening members. If the door frame is the split-jamb type that adjusts to fit different wall thicknesses, complete the installation by attaching the other half of the frame into the rough opening from the other side (**4**).

SEE ALSO

◁ Details for:

Hanging doors   58

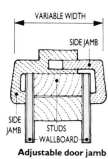

VARIABLE WIDTH

SIDE JAMB

SIDE JAMB

STUDS

WALLBOARD

Adjustable door jamb

JAMB   CASING

ROUGH OPENING

1 Install door

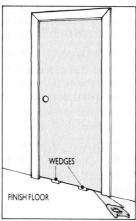

WEDGES

FINISH FLOOR

2 Trim with saw

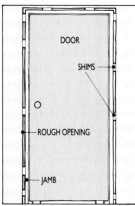

DOOR

SHIMS

ROUGH OPENING

JAMB

3 Shim out jambs

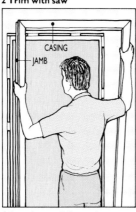

CASING

JAMB

4 Attach remaining casing

REPAIRING EXTERIOR DOOR FRAMES

Exterior door frames are built into the brickwork as it is erected, so replacing an old one means some damage to the plaster or the outside stucco.

In older houses, the frames are recessed into the brickwork, the inside face of the frame is flush with the plaster work and the architrave covers the joint. Modern houses may have frames close to or flush with the outer face of the brickwork. Work from the side the frame is closest to.

Measure the door and buy a standard frame to fit, or make one from standard frame sections.

Removing the old frame

Chop back the plaster or stucco with a chisel to expose the back face of the door frame (**1**).

With a general-purpose saw (**2**) cut through the three metal brackets holding the frame in the brickwork on each side, two about 9 inches from the top and bottom and one halfway up. Saw through the jambs halfway up (**3**), and if necessary cut the head member and the sill. Lever the frame members out with a crowbar.

Clear any loose material from the opening and repair a vertical vapor barrier in a cavity wall with gun-applied caulking to keep moisture out of the gap between inner and outer layers of brickwork.

Fitting the new frame

Fitting a frame is easier with its horns removed, but this weakens it. If possible, fit the frame with horns shaped like the old ones (see right).

Wedge the frame in position, checking that it is centered, square and plumb. Drill three counterbored clearance holes in each jamb for screws, positioned about 1 foot from the top and bottom with one halfway, but avoid drilling into mortar joints. Run a masonry drill through the clearance holes to mark their position on the brickwork.

Remove the frame, drill the holes in the brickwork and insert expandable metal wall plugs. Replace the frame and fix it with 4-inch steel screws. Plug the counterbores.

Pack any gap under the sill with mortar. Restore the brickwork, stucco or plasterwork and apply mastic sealant around the outer edge of the frame to seal any small gaps. Fit the door as described (◁).

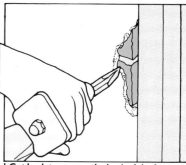

1 Cut back to expose the back of the frame

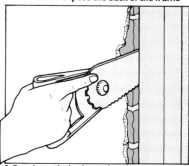

2 Cut through the frame brackets

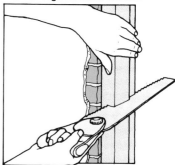

3 Saw through the frame to remove it

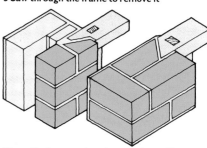

Shape the horns rather than cut them off

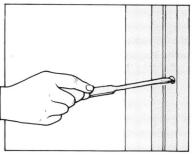

Screw the frame to the plugged wall

REPLACING A ROTTED FRAME

The great majority of exterior door frames are constructed of softwood, and this, if it is regularly maintained with good paint, will give years of excellent service. However, the ends of door sills and the frame posts are vulnerable to rot if they are subject to continual wetting. This can happen when the frame has moved because of shrinkage of the timber, or where old pointing has fallen out and left a gap where water can get in. Alternatively, old and porous brickwork or an ineffective moisture barrier can be the cause of moisture damage.

Prevention is always better than any cure, so check around the frame for any shrinkage gaps and apply a mastic sealant where necessary. Keep all pointing in good order. A slight outbreak of rot can be treated with the aid of a commercial repair kit and preservative.

It is possible for the sill to rot without the frame posts being affected. In this case, all you have to do is replace the sill. If the posts are also affected, repair them (see right). In some cases, the post ends can be tenoned into the sill and fitted as a unit.

Replacing a sill

You can buy 2 × 6 softwood or hardwood door sill sections that can be cut to the required length. If your sill is not of a standard-shaped section, the replacement can be made to order. It is more economical in the long run to specify a hardwood such as oak, as it will last much longer.

Taking out the old
First measure and note down the width of the door opening, then remove the door. Old jamb sides are usually tenoned into the sill, so to separate the sill from them, split it lengthwise with a wood chisel. A saw cut across the center of the sill can make the job of removing it easier.

The ends of the sills are set into the brickwork on either side, so cut away the bricks to make the removal of the old sill and insertion of the new one easier. Use a cold chisel to cut carefully through the mortar around the bricks, and try to preserve them for reuse after fitting the sill.

The new sill has to be inserted from the front so that it can be tucked under the jamb sides and into the brickwork. Cut the tenons off level with the shoulders of the jamb sides (**1**). Mark and cut shallow mortises for the ends of the jamb sides in the top of the new sill, spaced apart as previously noted. The mortises must be deep enough to take the full width of the jamb sides (**2**), which may mean the sill being slightly higher than the original one, so that you will have to trim a little off the bottom of the door.

Fitting the new
Try the new sill for fit and check that it is level. Before fastening it, apply a wood preservative to its underside and ends, and, as a moisture barrier, apply two or three coats of asphalt roofing sealer to the brickwork.

When both treatments are dry, glue the sill to the jamb sides, using an exterior woodworking adhesive. Wedge the underside of the sill with slate to push it up against the ends of the sides, toenail the sides to the sill and leave it for the adhesive to set.

Pack the gap between the underside of the sill and the masonry with a stiff mortar of 3 parts sand : 1 part cement, and rebond and point the bricks. Finish by treating the wood with preservative and applying a caulking sealant around the door frame.

1 Cut tenons off level with the joint's shoulder

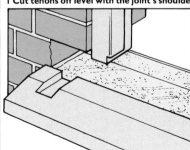

2 Cut a mortise to receive the side

REPAIRING DOOR POSTS

Rot can attack the ends of door posts, particularly in exposed positions where they meet stone steps or are set into concrete, as in some garages. The posts may be located on metal dowels set into the step.

If the damage is not too extensive, the rotted end can be cut away and replaced with a new piece, either scarf-jointed or half-lap-jointed into place. If your situation involves a wooden sill, combine the following information with that given for replacing a sill.

First remove the door, then saw off the end of the affected post back to sound wood. For a scarf joint, make the cut at 45 degrees to the face of the post (**1**). For a lap joint, cut it square. Chip any metal dowel out of the step with a cold chisel.

Measure and cut a matching section of post to the required length, allowing for the overlap of the joint, then cut the end to 45 degrees or mark and cut a half lap joint in both parts of the post (**2**).

Drill a hole in the end of the new section for the metal dowel if it is still usable. If it is not, make a new one from a piece of galvanized steel pipe, priming the metal to prevent corrosion. Treat the new wood with a preservative and insert the dowel. Set the dowel in mortar, at the same time gluing and screwing the joint (**3**).

If a dowel is not used, fix the post to the wall with counterbored screws. Place hardboard or plywood shims behind it if necessary and plug the counterbores of the screw holes.

Apply a caulk sealant to the joints between the door post, wall and base.

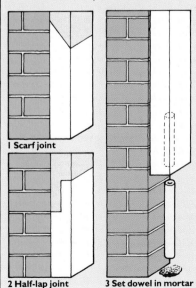

1 Scarf joint

2 Half-lap joint   **3 Set dowel in mortar**

- **Easing a sticking door**
If a door's bottom corner is rubbing on the frame, the door is probably swollen. Take it off its hinges and shave the corner with a plane. If the top corner is rubbing, first check the hinges. They may be so worn that the pins are slack and the door drops. Swap the hinges, top with bottom, to reverse wear on the pins, or install new hinges.

61

WINDOWS: TYPES AND CONSTRUCTION

The function of any window is to allow natural light into the house and to provide ventilation. Traditionally windows have been referred to as "lights", and the term "fixed light" is still used to describe a window or part of a window frame that doesn't open. A section that opens for ventilation, the "sash," is a separate frame that slides vertically or is hinged at its side, top or bottom edge. Windows of the hinged type are commonly referred to as casement windows.

A pane of glass can also be pivoted horizontally as a single sash, or several panes can be grouped together to make up a jalousie window.

Most window frames and sashes are made up from molded sections of solid wood. Clad-wood units offer the superior insulating properties and beauty of wood along with low maintenance. Steel and, more recently, aluminum or rigid vinyl frames are also used.

Casement windows

Window frames with hinged sashes—casement windows—are now produced in the widest range of materials and styles.

A traditional wooden window frame and its hinged sash are constructed in much the same way as a door and its frame. A jamb at each side is mortise-and-tenon jointed into the head member at the top and into a sill at the bottom (See below). The frame may be divided vertically by a "mullion", or horizontally by a "transom" (**1**).

The sash, which is carried by the frame, has its top and bottom rails jointed into its side stiles. Glazing bars, relatively light molded sections, are used to sub-divide the glazed area for smaller panes (**2**).

Side-hung sashes are fitted on butt hinges or sometimes, for better access to the outside of the glass, on "easy clean" extension hinges. A lever fastener, for securing the sash, is screwed to the middle of the stile on the opening side. A casement stay on the bottom rail holds the sash in various open positions and acts as a locking device when the sash is closed. Top-hung sashes, or vents, are secured with a stay only.

Galvanized-steel casement windows (**3**) were once popular for domestic use. They are made in the same format as wooden hinged windows but have a slimmer framework. The joints of the metal sections are welded.

Steel windows are strong and long-lasting but vulnerable to rust unless protected by galvanized plating or a good paint. The rusting can be caused by weathering outside or by condensation on the inside.

1 Casement window

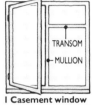
2 Glazing-bars

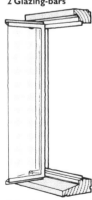
3 Steel casement type

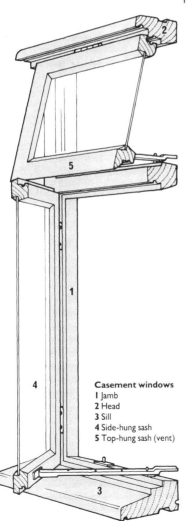

Casement windows
1 Jamb
2 Head
3 Sill
4 Side-hung sash
5 Top-hung sash (vent)

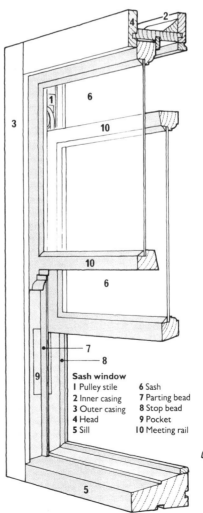

Sash window
1 Pulley stile	6 Sash
2 Inner casing	7 Parting bead
3 Outer casing	8 Stop bead
4 Head	9 Pocket
5 Sill	10 Meeting rail

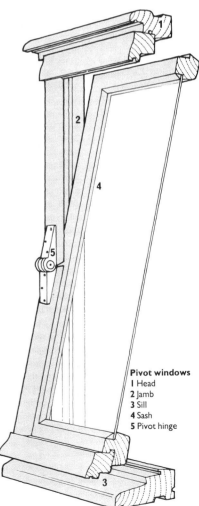

Pivot windows
1 Head
2 Jamb
3 Sill
4 Sash
5 Pivot hinge

WINDOWS: TYPES AND CONSTRUCTION

Sash windows

Vertically sliding windows are commonly known as sash windows and when both top and bottom sashes can be opened they are referred to as "double-hung" sash windows.

The traditional wooden type (see opposite) is constructed with a "box frame" in which the jambs are made up from three boards: the pulley stile, the inner casing and the outer casing. A back completes the box that houses the sash counterweights. The head is made up in a similar way but without the back lining, and the sill is of solid wood. The pulley stiles are jointed into the sill and the linings are set in a rabbet.

The sashes of a double-hung window are held in tracks formed by the jamb, a parting bead and an inner stop bead. The beads can be removed for servicing the sash mechanism. Each sash is counter-balanced by two cast-iron weights—one at each side—which are attached by strong cords or chains that pass over pulleys in the stiles. Access to the weights is through "pockets"—removable pieces of wood—set in the lower part of the stiles.

The top sash slides in the outer track and overlaps the inner bottom sash at their horizontal "meeting rails." The closing faces of the meeting rails are bevelled, and their wedging action helps to prevent the sashes rattling. It also provides better clearance when the window is opened and improves security when it is locked. The sashes are secured by two-part fasteners of various types fitted on the meeting rails.

Spiral balances

Modern wooden or aluminum vertically sliding sashes have spring-assisted spiral balances which do not need a deep box construction. Rather than being concealed, the slim balances are fitted on the faces of the stiles.

Spiral balances
The balances are usually fixed to the faces of the frame stiles and set in grooves in the sash stiles.

Pivot windows

Wooden-framed pivot windows (see opposite) are constructed in a similar way to casement windows, but the sash is held on a pair of strong pivot hinges which allow the window to be tilted right over for easy cleaning from inside. A safety roller arm can be fitted to the frame and set to prevent the window opening more than 4½ inches.

Pivoting roof windows are available for pitched roofs with slopes from 15- to 85-degrees. Like the standard pivoting windows, they can be fully reversed for cleaning. The windows are supplied double-glazed with sealed units; ventilators are incorporated in the frame or sash. The wood is protected on the outside by a metal covering. Flashing kits are supplied for installing in roofs.

Jalousie windows

A jalousie window is another form of pivot window. The jalousie are unframed "blades" of glass ⁵⁄₃₂ in. or ¼ in. thick, which have their long edges ground and polished. The panes are held at each end in light alloy carriers which pivot on an upright member, which is sometimes screwed to a wooden frame. One side is fitted with an opening and locking mechanism which links all of the panes so that they operate together as one.

Jalousie windows are effective as ventilators but they do not provide good security. They are also difficult to weatherseal.

Where an opening is more than 3 ft. 6 in. in width two sets of panes are best used, with the center pair of uprights set back-to-back in order to form a mullion.

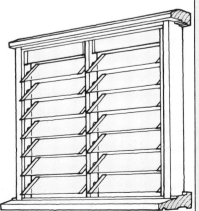

Use two sets of panes for a wide opening

ALUMINUM AND VINYL WINDOW FRAMES

Aluminum windows

These are now replacing old wooden and metal-framed windows. The aluminum is extruded into complex sections (1), to hold double-glazed sealed units and weather stripping and—ready finished in white, satin silver, black or bronze—is maintenance free. These windows are highly engineered and complete with concealed projection hinges and lockable fasteners. They need no stays to hold them open.

To combat condensation the latest designs incorporate a "thermal break" of insulating material in the hollow sections of the frame.

Most aluminum windows designed for replacement work are custom-made and fitted by contractors specializing in window installation.

Vinyl windows

Rigid vinyl windows (2) are similar to aluminum ones but are thicker through their sections. They are manufactured in white and brown, and once installed they require no maintenance.

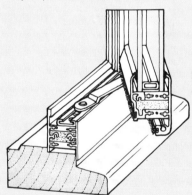

1 Extruded aluminum window set in wooden frame

2 Metal tube-reinforced extruded-vinyl window

SEE ALSO

Details for: ▷

| Replacement windows | 71-72 |

HOW WINDOWS ARE FITTED

Frame walls

Most new windows today are prefabricated and set into place as a single unit. Installing them is similar to installing doors.

First, measure the rough opening to be sure it is large enough to accept the window. Then, sheath all four sides of the opening with 15-pound building paper to prevent moisture damage **(1)**. Set the window into the opening from outside. Center it, then raise it on shims from the inside to the specified height.

Set a level on top of the sill and adjust the shims until the frame is both plumb and horizontal. From outside, carefully drive one finishing nail into an upper corner of the casing, partway into a stud. Start a nail in the opposite corner, check that the window frame is level, and drive the nail through the casing into the stud.

Measure between diagonal corners of the frame to be sure it is square, then insert shims between the side jambs to hold it in position. Nail the lower corners in place carefully **(2)**. After rechecking the frame for squareness, plumb and level, operate the sashes. If no further adjustment is necessary, finish nailing, trim shims flush, pack insulation between the window frame and rough opening from the inside, install a drip cap above the window, and caulk all seams to exclude moisture **(3)**.

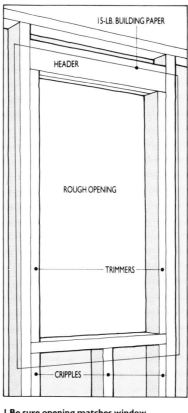

1 Be sure opening matches window
To narrow an opening, install extra trimmers or strips of plywood. Widen an opening by adding a new stud next to the framed opening and removing a trimmer. Alter the height of an opening by rebuilding the sill and lower cripples, not the header.

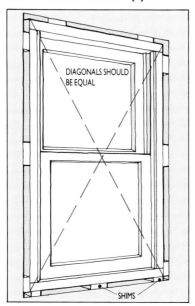

2 Tack window in place
Adjust with shims until all measurements are satisfactory and sash operates smoothly. Measurements taken between diagonals will be exactly equal if frame is square.

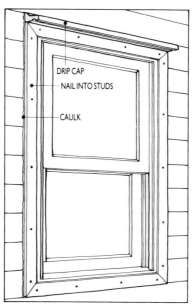

3 Nail through casing into studs only
Do not nail into sheathing. If necessary, pre-drill holes to prevent splitting. Attach drip cap to top of casing. Fill all nail holes with putty. Apply caulk around all four sides.

Masonry walls

In older brick houses it is usual to find the window frame jambs set in recesses on the inside of the brickwork. The openings were formed before the windows were fitted and the frames were nailed or screwed into wooden plugs in the brickwork. No vertical damp-proof courses were fitted. Evaporation was relied on to keep the walls dry.

The frames in a 9-inch-thick wall were set flush with the inside. Thicker walls had inner reveals. All required sub-sills, usually stone ones, outside.

Brickwork above the opening in a traditional brick wall may be supported by a brick arch or a stone lintel. Flat or shallow curved arches were generally used, their thickness being the width of one brick. Wooden lintels were placed behind such arches to support the rest of the wall's thickness. Semi-circular arches were usually as thick as the wall.

Many stone lintels were carved to make decorative features. As with arches, an inner lintel shared the weight. Openings like this were never wide because of the relative weakness of the materials. The wide windows of main rooms had several openings divided by brick or stone columns.

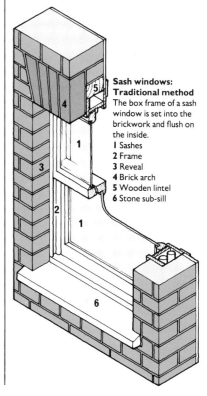

Sash windows: Traditional method
The box frame of a sash window is set into the brickwork and flush on the inside.
1 Sashes
2 Frame
3 Reveal
4 Brick arch
5 Wooden lintel
6 Stone sub-sill

BUYING GLASS

You can buy most types of glass from building supply and hardware stores. They will advise you on thickness, cut the glass to your measurements and also deliver larger sizes and amounts.

The thickness of glass, once expressed by weight, is now measured in inches. If you are replacing old glass, measure its thickness to the nearest 32nd, and, if it is slightly less than any available size, buy the next one up for the sake of safety.

Though there are no regulations about the thickness of glass, for safety reasons you should comply with the recommendations set out in the Uniform Building Code or your local code. The required thickness of glass depends on the area of the pane, its exposure to wind pressure and the vulnerability of its situation—e.g., in a window overlooking a play area. Tell your supplier what the glass is needed for—a door, a window, a shower screen, etc.—to ensure that you get the right type.

Measuring

Measure the height and width of the opening to the inside of the frame rabbet, taking the measurement from two points for each dimension. Also check that the diagonals are the same length. If they differ markedly and show that the frame is out of square, or if it is otherwise awkwardly shaped, make a cardboard template of it. In any case deduct ⅛ inch from the height and width to allow a fitting tolerance. When making a template allow for the thickness of the glass cutter.

When you order patterned glass, specify the height before the width. This will ensure that the glass is cut with the pattern running in the right direction. (Or take a piece of the old glass with you, which you may need to do in any case to match the pattern.)

For any asymmetrically shaped pane of patterned glass supply a template, and mark the surface that represents the outside face of the pane. This ensures that the glass will be cut with its smooth surface outside and will be easier to keep clean.

WORKING WITH GLASS

Always carry glass on its edge. You can hold it with pads of folded rag or paper to grip the top and bottom edge, though it is better to wear heavy working gloves.

Protect your hands with gloves and your eyes with goggles when removing broken glass from a frame. Wrap up the broken pieces in thick layers of newspaper if you have to dispose of them in your wastebasket, but before doing so check with your local glazier, who may be willing to take the pieces and add them to his cut-offs, to be sent back to the manufacturers for recycling.

Basic glass-cutting

It is usually unnecessary to cut your own glass as glass suppliers are willing to do it, but you may have surplus glass and want to cut it yourself. Diamond-tipped cutters are available, but the type with a steel wheel is cheaper and adequate for normal use.

Cutting glass successfully is largely a matter of practice and confidence. If you have not done it before, you should make a few practice cuts on waste pieces of glass and get used to the "feel" before doing a real job.

Lay the glass on a flat surface covered with a blanket. Patterned glass is placed patterned side down and cut on its smooth side. Clean the surface thoroughly.

Set a T-square the required distance from one edge, using a steel measuring tape (**1**). If you are working on a small piece of glass or do not have a T-square, mark the glass on opposite edges with a felt-tip pen or wax pencil. Use a straight edge to join up the marks and guide the cutter.

Lubricate the steel wheel of the glass cutter by dipping it in light machine oil or kerosene. Hold the cutter between middle finger and index finger (**2**) and draw it along the guide in one continuous stroke. Use even pressure throughout and run the cut off the end. Slide the glass forward over the edge of the table (**3**) and tap the underside of the scored line with the back of the cutter to initiate the cut. Grip the glass on each side of the score line with gloved hands (**4**), lift the glass and snap it in two. Alternatively, place a pencil under each end of the scored line and apply even pressure on both sides until the glass snaps.

1 Measure the glass with a tape and T-square

2 Cut glass in one continuous stroke

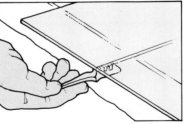
3 Tap the edge of glass to initiate the cut

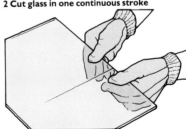
4 Snap glass in two

Cutting a thin strip of glass

A pane of glass may be slightly oversize due to inaccurate measuring or cutting or if the frame is distorted.

Remove a very thin strip of glass with the aid of a pair of pliers. Nibble away the edge by gripping the waste with the tip of the jaws close to the scored line.

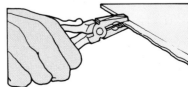
Nibble away a thin strip with pliers

REPAIRING A BROKEN WINDOW

A cracked window pane, even when no glass is missing from it, is a safety hazard and a security risk. If the window is actually lacking some of its glass, it is no longer weatherproof and should be repaired promptly.

Temporary repairs

For temporary protection from the weather, a sheet of polyethylene can be taped or pinned with strips over the outside of the window frame, and a cracked window can be temporarily repaired with a special clear self-adhesive waterproof tape. Applied to the outside, the tape gives an almost invisible repair.

Safety with glass

The method you use to remove the glass from a broken window will to some extent depend on conditions. If the window is not at ground level, it may be safest to take out the complete sash to do the job. But a fixed window will have to be repaired on the spot, where it is.

Large pieces of glass should be handled by two people and the work done from a scaffold rather than ladders. Avoid working in windy weather and always wear protective gloves for handling glass.

Repairing glass in wooden frames

In wooden window frames the glass is set into a rabbet cut in the frame's molding and bedded in linseed-oil putty. Small wedge-shaped nails called glazier's points are also used to hold the glass in place. In some wooden-framed windows a screwed-on beading is used to hold the pane instead of the "weathered" (outer) putty; this type of frame may have its rabbet cut on the inside instead of the outside.

Removing the glass

If the glass in a window pane has shattered, leaving jagged pieces set in the putty, grip each piece separately (wearing gloves) and try to work it loose (**1**). It is safest always to start working from the top of the frame.

Old dry putty will usually give way, but if it is strong it will have to be cut away with a glazier's hacking knife and a hammer (**2**). Alternatively, the job can be done with a blunt wood chisel. Work along the rabbet to remove the putty and glass. Pull out the points with pincers (**3**).

If the glass is cracked but not shattered, run a glass cutter around the perimeter of the pane about 1 inch from the frame, scoring the glass (**4**). Fasten strips of self-adhesive tape across the cracks and the scored lines (**5**) and tap each piece of glass so that it breaks free and is held only by the tape. Carefully peel the inner pieces away, then remove the pieces around the edges and the putty as described above.

Clean out the rabbet and seal it with a wood primer. Measure the height and width of the opening to the inside of the rabbets and have your new glass cut ⅛ inch smaller on each dimension to give a fitting tolerance.

Fitting new glass

Purchase new glazier's points and enough putty for the frame. Your glass supplier should be able to advise you on this but, as a guide, 1 pound of putty will fill about 13 linear feet.

Knead a palm-sized ball of putty to an even consistency. Very sticky putty is difficult to work with so wrap it briefly in newspaper to absorb some of the oil. You can soften putty that is too stiff by adding linseed oil to it.

Press a fairly thin, continuous band of putty into the rabbet all around with your thumb. This is the bedding putty. Lower the edge of the new pane on to the bottom rabbet, then press it into the putty. Press close to the edges only, squeezing the putty to leave a bed about 1/16 inch behind the glass, then secure the glass with points about 8 inches apart. Tap them into the frame with the edge of a firmer chisel so that they lie flat with the surface of the glass (**1**). Trim the surplus putty from the back of the glass with a putty knife.

Apply more putty to the rabbet all around, outside the glass. With a putty knife (**2**), work the putty to a smooth finish at an angle of 45 degrees. Wet the knife with water to prevent it dragging and make neat miters in the putty at the corners. Let the putty set and stiffen for about three weeks, then apply an oil-based undercoat paint. Before painting, clean any putty smears from the glass with paint remover. Let the paint lap the glass slightly to form a weather seal.

A self-adhesive plastic foam can be used instead of the bedding putty. Run it around the back of the rabbet in a continuous strip, starting from a top corner, press the glass into place on the foam and secure it with points. Then apply the weathered putty in the same way described above. Alternatively, apply a strip of foam around the outside of the glass and cover it with a wooden beading, then paint.

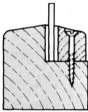

Weathered putty

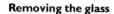
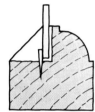

Wooden bead
Unscrew beading and scrape out mastic. Bed new glass in fresh astic and replace beading.

I Work loose the broken glass

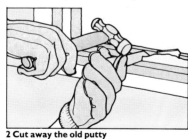

2 Cut away the old putty

3 Pull out the old points

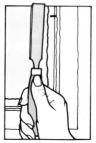

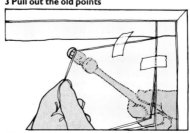

I Tap in new points

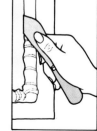

2 Shape the putty

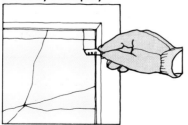

4 Score glass before removing a cracked pane

5 Tap the glass to break it free

REPAIRING ROTTED FRAMES

Softwood is the traditional material for making wooden window frames, and providing it is of sound quality and is well cared for, it will last the life of the building.

New frames or frames that have been stripped should always be treated with a clear wood preservative before being primed and painted.

Regular maintenance
It is the bottom rail of a wooden window frame that is most vulnerable to rot if it is not protected. The water may be absorbed by the wood through a poor paint finish or by penetrating behind old shrunken putty. An annual check of all window frames should be carried out and any faults should be dealt with. Old putty that has shrunk away from the glass should be cut out and replaced.

Remove old, flaking paint, repair any cracks in the wood with a flexible filler and repaint, ensuring that the underside of the sash is well painted.

Replacing a sash rail

Where rot is well advanced and the rail is beyond repair, it should be cut out and replaced. This should be done before the rot spreads to the stiles of the frame. Otherwise you will eventually have to replace the whole sash frame.

Remove the sash either by unscrewing the hinges or—if it is a double-hung sash window—by removing the beading.

With a little care the repair can be carried out without the glass being removed from the sash frame, though if the window is large it would be safer to take out the glass. In any event, cut away the putty from the damaged rail.

The bottom rail is tenoned into the stiles (**1**), but it can be replaced by using bridle joints. Saw down the shoulder lines of the tenon joints (**2**) from both faces of the frame and remove the rail.

Make a new rail, or buy a piece if it is a standard section, and mark and cut it to length with a full-width tenon at each end. Set the positions of the tenons to line up the mortises of the stiles. Cut the shoulders to match the rabbeted sections of the stiles (**3**) or, if it has a decorative molding, pare the molding away to leave a flat shoulder (**4**).

Cut slots in the ends of the stiles to receive the tenons.

Glue the new rail into place with a waterproof resin adhesive and reinforce the two joints with pairs of ¼-inch dowels. Drill the stopped holes from the inside of the frame and stagger them for greater rigidity.

When the adhesive is dry, plane the surface as required and treat the new wood with a clear preservative. Reputty the glass and paint the new rail within three weeks.

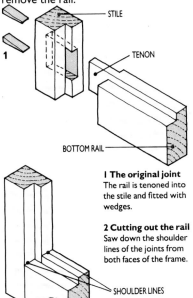

1 The original joint
The rail is tenoned into the stile and fitted with wedges.

2 Cutting out the rail
Saw down the shoulder lines of the joints from both faces of the frame.

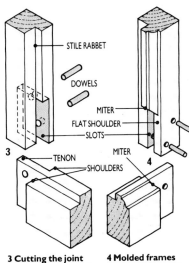

3 Cutting the joint
Cut tenons at each end of the rail with the shoulders matching the sections of the stiles.

4 Molded frames
Pare away the molding of the stile to receive the square shoulder of the rail. Miter the molding.

REPLACING A FIXED-LIGHT RAIL

The frames of some fixed lights are made like sashes but are screwed to the main frame jamb and mullion. Such a frame can be repaired in the same way as a sash (see left) after its glass is removed and it is unscrewed from the window frame. Where this proves too difficult, you will have to carry out the repair in place.

First remove the putty and the glass, then saw through the rail at each end. With a chisel, trim the rabbeted edge of the jamb(s) and/or mullion to a clean surface at the joint (**1**) and chop out the old tenons. Cut a new length of rail to fit between the prepared edges and cut mortises in its top edge at both ends to take loose tenons. Place the mortises so that they line up with the mortises in the stiles and make them twice as long as the depth of those mortises.

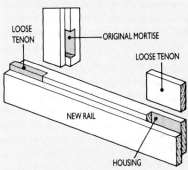

1 Cut the tenons and trim a new rail to fit

Cut two loose tenons to fit the rail mortises, and two packing pieces. The latter should have one sloping edge (**2**).

Apply waterproof woodworking adhesive to all of the joint surfaces, place the rail between the frame members, insert the loose tenons and push them sideways into the stile mortises. Drive the packing pieces behind the tenons to lock them in place. When the adhesive has set, trim the top edges, treat the new wood with clear preservative, replace the glass and reputty. Paint within three weeks.

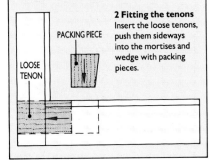

2 Fitting the tenons
Insert the loose tenons, push them sideways into the mortises and wedge with packing pieces.

● **Removing glass**
Removing glass from a window frame in one piece is not easy, so be prepared for it to break. Apply adhesive tape across the glass to bind the pieces together if it should break. Chisel away the putty to leave a clean rabbet, then pull out the points. Work the blade of a putty knife into the bedding joint on the inside of the frame to break the grip of the putty. Steady the glass and lift it out when it becomes free.

REPAIRING ROTTED SILLS

The sill is a fundamental part of a window frame, and one attacked by rot can mean major repair work.

A window frame is constructed in the same way as a door frame and can be repaired in a similar way. All the glass should be removed first, preferably by removing the sashes. Be sure to check the condition of the subsill (part of the rough frame). Rot can extend into this region also if the opening was not covered with building paper. After repairs have been made, be careful to thoroughly weatherseal the window frame to prevent moisture from entering once again. Reapply fresh 15-pound asphalt-saturated building paper around exposed parts of the rough frame, then caulk all seams where the window frame itself contacts the exterior of the house. Repairing sills is difficult and time-consuming, so plan to do such work during warm weather when window openings can be covered with polyethylene while work progresses.

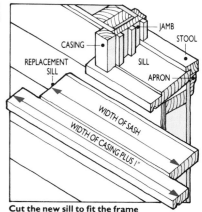

Double-hung window in frame wall

Replacing a wooden sill

Ideally, to replace a rotted window sill you should remove the entire window, carefully disassemble the old sill from the jamb sides, use it as a template, then cut and fit a new sill and replace the window. However, sills may be replaced with the window in place, provided you work patiently and have some skill at scribing and shaping wood with a chisel. Begin by carefully splitting out the old sill. Cut through it crosswise in two places with a saw to remove the middle portion, then gently pry the end sections away from the jambs. Hacksaw any nails holding the sill to the rest of the frame.

Use a piece of cardboard to make a template for a new sill, shaped to fit between the jambs but beneath the casing on the outside. Cut a 10-degree bevel along the upper outside edge of the sill, extending to the inside edge of the sash, then bevel the sash area so it is level when the sill is installed. Fill the area beneath the sill with insulation, install the sill with 16d finishing nails, then thoroughly caulk the seams.

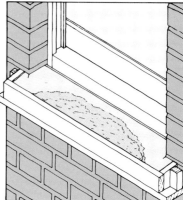

Cut the new sill to fit the frame

Repairing a stone subsill

• Relieving sticking windows
In wet weather, the sashes of wooden casement windows may swell and bind in the frame. If the windows have not been well painted, wait for the wood to shrink in dry weather, then apply a good paint. An excessive paint build-up may cause a casement window to stick in any weather. Strip the old paint from the meeting edges of the sash and/or the frame rabbet and apply fresh paint.

The traditional stone sills featured in older houses may become eroded by the weather if they are not protected with paint. They may also suffer cracking due to subsidence in part of the wall.

Repair any cracks and eroded surfaces with a quick-setting waterproof cement. Rake the cracks out to clean and enlarge them, then dampen the stone with clean water and work the cement well into the cracks, finishing off flush with the top surface.

Depressions caused by erosion should be undercut to provide the cement with a good hold. A thin layer of cement simply applied to a shallow depression in the surface will not last. Use a cold chisel to cut away the surface of the sill at least 1 inch below the finished level and remove all traces of dust.

Make a wooden form to the shape of the sill and temporarily nail it to the brickwork. Dampen the stone, pour in the cement and tamp it level with the form, then smooth it with a trowel. Leave it to set for a couple of days before removing the form. Let it dry thoroughly before painting.

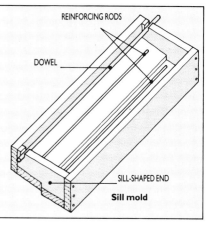

Make a wooden form to the shape of the sill

CASTING A NEW SUBSILL

Cut out the remains of the old stone sill with a hammer and cold chisel. Make a wooden mold with its end pieces shaped to the same section as the old sill. The mold must be made upside down, its open top representing the underside of the sill.

Fill two thirds of the mold with fine ballast concrete, tamped down well, and then add two lengths of mild steel reinforcing rod, judiciously spaced to share the volume of the sill, then fill the remainder of the mold. Set a narrow piece of wood such as a dowel into notches previously cut in the ends of the mold. This is to form a "throat" or drip groove in the underside of the sill.

Cover the concrete with polyethylene sheeting or dampen it regularly for two or three days to prevent rapid drying. When the concrete is set (allow about seven days), remove it from the mold and re-lay the sill in the wall on a bed of mortar to meet the wooden sill.

RE-CORDING A SASH WINDOW

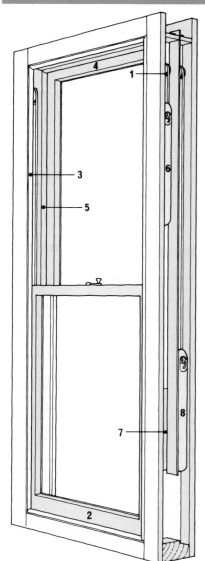

The workings of a double-hung sash window

1 Pulleys	5 Parting bead
2 Bottom sash	6 Bottom sash weight
3 Stop bead	7 Pocket
4 Top sash	8 Top sash weight

The sash cording from which the sashes are suspended will wear and in time will break. You should replace both cords even when only one has broken.

Waxed sash cording is normally sold in standard hanks, though some suppliers sell it by the foot. Each sash will require two lengths about three-quarters the height of the window. Sash chain is more durable than cord.

Removing the sashes

Lower the sashes and cut through the cords with a knife to release the weights. Hold on to the cords and lower the weights as far as possible before letting them drop. Pry off the side stop beads from inside the frame, starting in the middle and bowing them to make their mitered ends spring out and avoid breakage.

Lean the inner sash forward and mark the ends of the cord grooves on the face of the sash stiles. Reposition the sash and transfer the marks onto the pulley stiles (1). The sash can now be pulled clear of the frame.

Carefully pry out the two parting beads from their grooves in the stiles. The top sash can then be removed, after marking the ends of the grooves as before. Place sashes safely aside.

To gain access to the weights, take out the pocket pieces which were trapped by the parting bead and lift the weights out through the openings. Hanging pieces of thin wood known as parting strips may be fitted inside the box stiles to keep the pairs of weights apart. Push these aside to reach the outer weights.

Remove the old cord from the weights and sashes and clean them up ready for the new sash cords.

Fitting the sashes

The top sash is fitted first, but not before all of the sash cords and weights are in place. Clean away any buildup of paint from the pulleys. Tie a length of fine string to one end of the sash cord. Weight the other end of the string with small nuts or a piece of chain. Thread the weight—known as a mouse—over a pulley (2) and pull the string through the pocket opening until the cord is pulled through. Attach the end of the cord to a weight with a special knot (see below left).

Use the sash marks to measure the length of cord required. Pull on the cord to hoist the weight up to the pulley. Then let it drop back about 4 inches. Hold it temporarily in this position with a nail driven into the stile just below the pulley. Cut the cord level with the mark on the pulley stile (3).

Repeat this procedure for the cord on the other side, and then for the bottom sash.

Replace the top sash on the sill, removing the temporary nails in turn. Lean the sash forward, locate the cords into the grooves in the stiles and nail them in place using three or four 1-inch round wire nails. Nail only the bottom 6 inches, not all the way up (4). Lift the sash to check that the weights do not touch bottom.

Replace the pocket pieces and nail the parting beads in their grooves. Fit the bottom sash in the same way. Finally, replace the stop beads; take care to position them accurately.

SEE ALSO	
Details for: ▷	
Spiral balances	63, 70
Replacement windows	71-72

• Curing rattling windows
Casement window rattling is usually caused by an ill-fitting lever fastener. Replace a worn fastener, or reset the plate on the frame into which the fastener fits. The cause of wooden-sash window rattling is usually a bottom sash that fits loosely in its stile tracks. Replace the inner stop bead with a new length so that it makes a close fit against the sash. Rub candle wax on both sliding surfaces.

HOW TO TIE A SASH WEIGHT KNOT

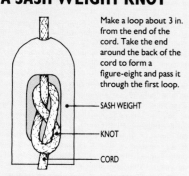

Make a loop about 3 in. from the end of the cord. Take the end around the back of the cord to form a figure-eight and pass it through the first loop.

— SASH WEIGHT
— KNOT
— CORD

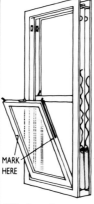

1 Mark cord grooves

MARK HERE

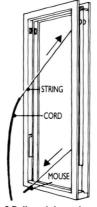

STRING
CORD
MOUSE

2 Pull cord through

CUT HERE

3 Cut cords at mark

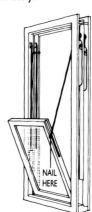

NAIL HERE

4 Nail cord to sash

SPIRAL BALANCES

Instead of cords and counterweights, modern sash windows use spiral balances which are mounted on the faces of the frame stiles, eliminating the need for traditional box sections. The balances are made to order to match the size and weight of individual glazed sashes and can be ordered through building supply stores or by mail.

Spiral balance components

Each balance consists of a torsion spring and a spiral rod housed in a tube. The top end is fixed to the stile and the inner spiral to the bottom of the sash. The complete unit can be housed in a groove in the sash stile or in the jamb of the frame.

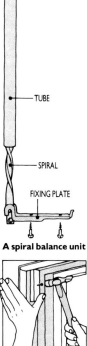

TUBE

SPIRAL

FIXING PLATE

A spiral balance unit

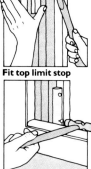

Fit top limit stop

Fit bottom limit stop

Sash window fitted with balances
1 Top limit stop
2 Top sash balance
3 Bottom sash balance
4 Fixing plate
5 Fixing plate
6 Bottom limit stop
7 Top sash
8 Bottom sash

Fitting the balances

You can fit spiral sash balances to replace the weights in a traditionally constructed sash window.

Remove the sashes and weigh them on your bathroom scales. Place your order, giving the weight of each sash and its height and width, also the height of the frame. Refit the sashes temporarily until the balances arrive, then take them out again and remove the pulleys.

Plug the holes and paint the stiles. Cut grooves, as specified by the manufacturers, in the stiles of each sash, to take the balances (1). Cut a mortise at each end of their bottom edges to receive the spiral rod mounting plates. Fit the plates with screws (2).

Sit the top sash in place, resting it on the sill, and fit the parting bead. Take the top pair of balances, which are shorter than those for the bottom sash, and locate each in its groove (3). Fix the top ends of the balance tubes to the frame stiles with the screw nails provided (4) and set the ends tight against the head.

Lift the sash to its full height and prop it with a length of wood. Hook the wire "key," provided by the makers, into the hole in the end of each spiral rod and pull each one down about 6 inches. Keeping the tension on the spring, add three to five turns counterclockwise (5). Locate the ends of the rods in the mounting plate and test the balance of the sash. If it drops, add another turn on the springs until it is just held in position. Take care not to overwind the balances.

Fit the bottom sash in the same way, refitting the staff bead to hold it in place. Fit the stops that limit the full travel of the sashes in their respective tracks (see left).

RENOVATING SPIRAL BALANCES

In time the springs of spiral balances may weaken. Retension them by unhooking the spiral rods from the mounting plates, then turning the rods counterclockwise once or twice.

The mechanisms can be serviced by releasing the tension and unwinding the rods from the tubes. Wipe them clean and apply a little thin oil, then rewind the rods back into the tubes and tension them as described above.

1 Cut a groove in the sash stiles

2 Fix the plates in their mortises with screws

3 Fit the sash and locate the tube in its groove

4 Nil the top end of the tube to the stile

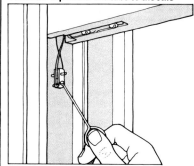

5 Tension the springs with the key provided

READY-MADE WINDOWS

Building suppliers offer a range of ready-made window frames in wood, vinyl and aluminum, and some typical examples are shown below.

Unfortunately, the range of sizes is rather limited, but where a ready-made frame is fairly close to one's requirements, it is possible to alter the size of the window's rough opening by cutting out or adding frame pieces, as described on page 198. In a wall of exposed brickwork, the window frame should be made to measure.

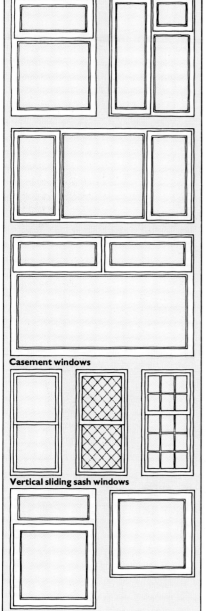

Casement windows

Vertical sliding sash windows

Pivot windows

REPLACEMENT WINDOWS

The style of the windows is an important element in the appearance of any house. Should you be thinking of replacing windows in an older dwelling you might find it better—and not necessarily more expensive—to have new wooden frames made rather than to change to modern windows of aluminum or vinyl.

Planning and building regulations

Window conversions do not normally need planning permission, as they come under the heading of home improvement or home maintenance. But if you plan to alter your windows significantly—for example, by bricking one up or making a new window opening, or both—you should consult your local building inspector.

All codes have certain minimum requirements, some pertaining to ventilation and some to the ratio of glass area to floor space.

You should also find out from your local authority if you live in a historic section, which could mean some limitation on your choice.

Buying replacement windows

Custom woodworking mills will make up wooden window frames to your size. Specify hardwood or, for a painted finish, softwood impregnated with a preservative.

Alternatively, you can approach one of the replacement window companies, though this is likely to limit your choice to aluminum or vinyl frames. The ready-glazed units can be fitted to your present framing or to new framing, should alteration be necessary. Most of the replacement window companies operate on the basis of supplying and also fitting the windows, and their service includes disposing of the old windows after removal.

This method saves time and labor, but you should carefully compare the various offerings of these companies and their compatibility with the style of your house before opting for one. Choose a frame that reproduces, as closely as possible, the proportions of the original window.

Replacing a casement window

Measure the width and height of the window opening. Windows in brick masonry will need a wood subframe. If the existing one is in good condition, take your measurements from inside the frame. Otherwise, take them from the brickwork. You may have to cut away some of the stucco first to get accurate measurements. Order the replacement window accordingly.

Remove the old window by first taking out the sashes and then the panes of glass in any fixed part. Unscrew the exposed hardware, such as may be found in a metal frame, or pry the parts of the frame out and cut through fasteners with a hacksaw. It should be possible to knock the frame out in one piece, but if not, saw through it in several places and lever the pieces out with a crowbar (1). Clean up the exposed masonry with a bricklayer's chisel to make a neat opening.

1 Lever out the pieces of the old frame

Cut the horns off the new frame if present, then plumb the frame in the window opening and wedge it (2). Drill screw holes through the stiles into the rough frame or masonry (3). Refit the frame, checking again that it is plumb before screwing it home.

Patch the wall on both sides if necessary. Gaps of ¼ inch or less can be filled with caulk. Glaze the new frame as required.

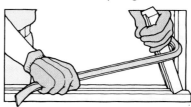

2 Fit the new frame   **3 Drill screw holes**

SEE ALSO	
Details for:▷	
Window types	63
Fitting windows	64
Removing sashes	69

REPLACEMENT WINDOWS

Bay windows

A bay window is a combination of window frames which are built out from the face of the building. The side frames may be set at 90-, 60- or 45-degree angles to the front of the house. Curved bays are also made with equal-sized frames set at a very slight angle to each other to form a faceted curve.

The frames of a bay window are set on framing which is built to the shape of the bay, which may be at ground level only, with a flat or pitched roof, or may be continued up through all stories and finished with a gabled roof.

Bay windows in brick homes can break away from the main wall through subsidence caused by a poor foundation or differential ground movements. Damage from slight movements can be repaired once the ground has stabilized. Repoint the brickwork and apply mastic sealant to gaps around the woodwork. Damage from extensive or persistent movement should be dealt with by a builder. Consult your local building inspector and inform your homeowners insurance company.

Fitting the frame

Where the height of the original window permits it, standard window frames can be used to make up a replacement bay window. Using gasket seals, various combinations of frames can be arranged. Shaped hardwood corner posts are available to give a 90-, 60- or 45-degree angle to the side frames. The gasket is used for providing a weatherproof seal between the posts and the frames.

SEE ALSO

◁ Details for:
Removing sashes	69
Window types	63

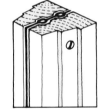

Joining frames
A flexible gasket, which is sold by the foot, is available for joining standard frames. The frames are screwed together to fit the opening.

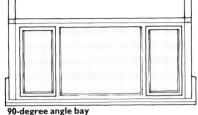

90-degree angle bay

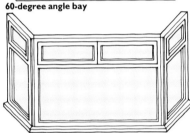
60-degree angle bay

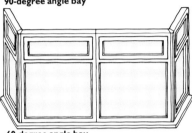

45-degree angle bay

Hardwood bay window (detail)

Bow windows

These are windows constructed on a shallow curve, and they normally project from a flat wall. Complete bow window frames are available from window manufacturers, ready for installation. Bow windows can be substituted for conventional ones.

To install, build out the rough opening as necessary, cutting back the siding to receive the exterior trim if the window is precased. Center the window in the opening, shim it plumb and level, then nail it into place. Install purchased braces or ones you build yourself beneath the window to support it. Also, install a canopy to shed rain and snow from the top. Add flashing and new siding where necessary, then caulk all seams. Pack insulation between the window frame and rough opening from the inside, then install interior trim.

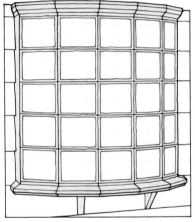
Bow window with braces

REPLACING A SASH WINDOW IN BRICK

An old vertically sliding sash window with cords and counterweights can be replaced with a new frame fitted with spiral balance sashes.

Remove the sashes (◁), then take out the old frame from inside the room. Pry off the casing, then the window jamb, and chop away the plaster as necessary. Most frames make a wedge fit, and you can loosen one by hitting the sill on the outside with a heavy hammer and a wood block. Lift the frame out of the opening when it is loose (**I**) and remove any debris from the opening once the window has been removed.

Set the new frame centrally in the opening so that its stiles are showing equal amounts on each side of the exterior brickwork reveals. Check the frame for plumb and wedge the corners at the head and the sill. Make up the space left by the old box stiles with mortared brickwork (**2**).

Metal brackets screwed to the frame's stiles can also be set in the mortar bed joints to secure the frame.

When the mortar is set, replaster the inner wall and replace the casing. In the meantime, glaze the sashes. Finally, apply a caulk sealant to the joints between the outside brickwork and the frame to keep the weather out.

I Lift out old frame   **2 Fill gaps with brick**

BUILDING CODES AND PERMITS

Building codes

Building codes are comprehensive guidelines intended to set standards for construction practices and material specifications. Their purpose is to ensure the adequate structural and mechanical performance, fire safety and overall quality of buildings and to address health and environmental concerns related to the way buildings are constructed. By setting minimum standards, building codes also limit unfair competitive practices among contractors.

Building codes address nearly every detail of building construction from the acceptable recipes for concrete used in the foundation to the permissible fire rating of the roof finish material—and many features in between. Partly because codes attempt to be as comprehensive as possible and also because they must address different concerns in varied locales, they are very lengthy, complex and lack uniformity from region to region. A further complication is that many new building products become available each year that are not accounted for in existing codes. Model codes promulgated by four major organizations are widely used for reference throughout the United States.

The Uniform Building Code, published by the International Conference of Building Officials, is perhaps the most widely accepted code. ICBO republishes the entire code every three years and publishes revisions annually. A short form of the Uniform Building Code covering buildings with less than three stories and less than 6,000 square feet of ground floor area is available—easier for home builders, and remodelers' reference.

The BOCA-Basic Building Code, issued by the Building Officials and Code Administrators International, Inc., is also widely used. An abridged form designed for residential construction, which includes plumbing and wiring standards, is available.

A third model code, prepared under the supervision of the American Insurance Association and known as the National Building Code, serves as the basis for codes adopted by many communities. It, too, is available in a short form for matters related to home construction.

The Standard Building Code is published by the Southern Building Code Congress International, Inc. It addresses conditions and problems prevalent in the southern United States.

While it is likely that one of the model codes named above serves as the basis for the building code in your community, municipal governments and states frequently add standards and restrictions. It is your local building department that ultimately decides what is acceptable and what is not. Consult that agency if a code question should arise.

Building codes are primarily designed for the safety of the building occupants and the general welfare of the community at large. It is wise to follow *all* practices outlined by the prevailing code in your area.

Building permits

A building permit is generally required for new construction, remodeling projects that involve structural changes or additions, and major demolition projects. In some locales it may be necessary to obtain a building permit for constructing in-ground pools, and you may need a building permit or rigger's license to erect scaffolding as an adjunct to nonstructural work on a house.

To obtain a building permit, you must file forms prescribed by your local building department that answer questions about the proposed site and project. In addition, it is necessary to file a complete set of drawings of the project along with detailed specifications. A complete set normally includes a plot plan or survey, foundation plan, floor plans, wall sections and electrical, plumbing and mechanical plans. Building permit fees are usually assessed based on the estimated cost of construction and records of the application are usually passed along to the local tax department for reassessment of the property value.

At the time you apply for a building permit, you may be advised of other applications for official permission that are required. For example, you may need to apply to the county health department concerning projects that may affect sewerage facilities and natural water supplies. It is important to arrange inspections in a timely way since finish stages cannot proceed until the structural, electrical, plumbing and mechanical work are approved.

Anyone may apply for a building permit, but it is usually best to have an architect or contractor file in your behalf, even if you plan to do the work yourself.

Zoning restrictions

Even for projects that do not require a building permit, local zoning regulations may limit the scope and nature of the construction permitted. Whereas building codes and permit regulations relate to a building itself, zoning rules address the needs and conditions of the community as a whole by regulating the development and uses of property. Zoning restrictions may apply to such various cases as whether a single-family house can be remodeled into apartments, whether a commercial space can be converted to residential use or the permissible height of a house or outbuilding.

It is advisable to apply to the local zoning board for approval before undertaking any kind of construction or remodeling that involves a house exterior or yard or if the project will substantially change the way a property is used. If the project does not conform with the standing zoning guidelines, you may apply to the zoning board for a variance. It is best to enlist the help of an architect or attorney for this.

Landmark regulations

Homes in historic districts may be subject to restrictions placed to help the neighborhood retain its architectural distinction and character. For the most part in designated landmark areas, changes in house exteriors are closely regulated. While extensive remodeling that would significantly change the architectural style are almost never permitted, even seemingly small modifications of existing structures are scrutinized. For example, metal or vinyl replacement windows may not be permitted for Victorian homes in designated areas, or the exterior paint and roof colors may be subject to approval. Even the color of the mortar used to repoint brickwork may be specified by the local landmarks commission or similar regulating body. Designs for new construction must conform to the prevalent architectural character. If you live in an historic district, it is advised that you apply to the governing body for approval of any plans for exterior renovation.

73

WILL YOU NEED A PERMIT OR VARIANCE?

Building code requirements and zoning regulations vary from city to city and frequently have county and state restrictions added to them. For this reason, it is impossible to state categorically which home-improvement projects require official permission and which do not. The chart below, which lists some of the most frequently undertaken projects, is meant to serve as a rough guide. Taken as a whole, it suggests a certain logic for anticipating when and what type of approval may be needed. Whether or not official approval is required, all work should be carried out in conformity with local code standards.

TYPE OF WORK	BUILDING PERMIT NEEDED		ZONING APPROVAL NEEDED	
 Exterior painting and repairs Interior decoration and repairs	NO	Permit or rigger's license may be needed to erect exterior scaffolding	NO	Certificate of appropriateness may be needed in historic areas
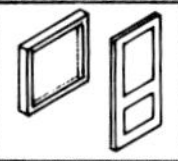 Replacing windows and doors	NO		NO	Permissible styles may be restricted in historic districts
 Electrical	NO	Have work performed or checked by a licensed contractor	NO	Outdoor lighting may be subject to approval
 Plumbing	NO	Have work performed or checked by a licensed contractor	NO	Work involving new water supply, septic or sewerage systems may require county health department
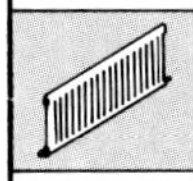 Heating	NO		NO	Installation of new oil storage tanks may require state environmental agency approval
 Constructing patios and decks	Possibly		Possibly	
Installing a hot tub	NO		NO	
 Structural alterations	YES		NO	Unless alterations change building height above limit or proximity of building to lot line
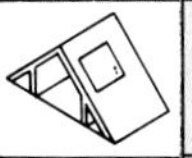 Attic remodeling	NO	Ascertain whether joists can safely support the floor load	NO	
 Building a fence or garden wall	NO		YES	In cases where structure is adjacent to public road or easement or extends above a height set by board
 Planting a hedge	NO		NO	
 Path or sidewalk paving	NO		Possibly	Public sidewalks must conform to local standards and specifications
 Clearing land	NO		YES	County and state environmental approval may also be needed
 Constructing an in-ground pool	YES		YES	County and state environmental approval may also be needed
 Constructing outbuildings	YES	For buildings larger than set limit	Possibly	
 Adding a porch	NO	Unless larger than set limit	Possibly	Regulations often set permissible setback from public road
 Adding a sunspace or greenhouse	YES		Possibly	Yes, if local rules apply to extensions
 Constructing a garage	YES		Possibly	Yes, if used for a commercial vehicle and within set proximity to lot line
 Driveway paving	NO		Possibly	Yes where access to public road created, also restrictions on proximity to lot lines
 Constructing a house extension	YES		Possibly	Regulations may limit permissible house size and proximity to lot lines
 Demolition	YES	If work involves structural elements	NO	Structures in historic districts may be protected by regulations
 Converting 1-family house to multi-unit dwelling	YES	Fire safety and ventilation codes are frequently more stringent for multiple dwellings	YES	
 Converting a residential building to commercial use	YES		YES	

74

BUILDER'S TOOL KIT

Bricklayers, carpenters and plasterers are all specialist builders, each requiring a set of specific tools, but the amateur is more like one of the self-employed builders who must be able to tackle several areas of building work, and so need a much wider range of tools than the specialist. The builder's tool kit suggested here is for renovating and improving the structure of a house and for erecting and restoring garden structures or paving.

LEVELING AND MEASURING TOOLS

You can make several specialized tools for measuring and leveling, but don't skimp on essentials like a good level and a strong tape measure.

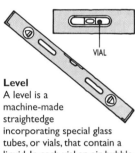

Level

A level is a machine-made straightedge incorporating special glass tubes, or vials, that contain a liquid. In each vial an air bubble floats. When a bubble rests exactly between two lines marked on the glass, the structure on which the level is held is known to be exactly horizontal or vertical, depending on the vial's orientation. Buy a wooden or lightweight aluminum level 2 to 3 feet long. A well-made one is very strong, but treat it with care and always clean mortar or plaster from it before the material sets.

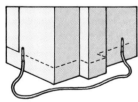

Water level

You can make a water level from a garden hose with short lengths of transparent plastic tube plugged into its ends. Fill the hose with water until it appears in both tubes. As water level is constant, the levels in the tubes are always identical and so can be used for marking identical heights even over long distances and around obstacles and bends.

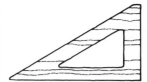

Builder's square

A large set square is useful when you set out brick or concrete-block corners. The best ones are stamped out of sheet metal, but you can make a serviceable one by cutting out a thick plywood right-angled triangle with a hypotenuse of about 2 feet 6 inches. Cut out the center of the triangle to reduce the weight.

Checking a square

Accuracy is important, so check the square by placing it against a straight strip of wood on the floor, drawing a line against the square to make a right angle with the strip, then turning the square to see if it forms the same angle from the other side.

Try square

Use a try square for marking out square cuts or joints on timber.

Making a plumb line

Any small but heavy weight hung on a length of line or string will make a suitable plumb line for judging the verticality of structures or surfaces.

Bricklayer's line

Use a bricklayer's line as a guide for laying bricks or blocks level. It is a length of nylon string stretched between two flat-bladed pins that are driven into vertical joints at the ends of a wall. There are also special line blocks that hook over the bricks at the ends of a course. As an improvisation, you can stretch a string between two stakes driven into the ground outside the line of the wall.

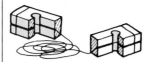

Line blocks

Blocks grip the brickwork corners; the line passes through their slots.

Plasterer's rule

A plasterer's rule is simply a straight wooden strip used for scraping plaster and rendering undercoats level.

Straightedge

Any length of straight, fairly stout lumber can be used to tell whether a surface is flat or, used with a level, to test whether two points are at the same height.

Gauge stick

For gauging the height of brick courses, calibrate a wooden strip by making saw cuts across it at 3-inch intervals—the thickness of a brick plus its mortar joint.

Tape measure

An ordinary retractable steel tape measure is adequate for most purposes, but if you need to mark out or measure a large plot, rent a wind-up tape up to 100 feet in length.

Marking gauge

This tool has a sharp steel point for scoring a line on lumber parallel to its edge. Its adjustable stock acts as a fence and keeps the point a constant distance from the edge.

FLOATS AND TROWELS

For professional builders, floats and trowels have specific uses, but in home maintenance, the small trowel for repointing brickwork is often ideal for patching small areas of plaster, while the plasterer's trowel is as likely to be used for smoothing concrete.

Brick trowel

A brick trowel is for handling and placing mortar when laying bricks or concrete blocks. A professional might use one with a blade as long as 1 foot, but such a trowel is too heavy and unwieldy for the amateur, so buy a good-quality brick trowel with a short blade.

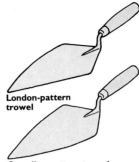

London-pattern trowel

Canadian-pattern trowel

The blade of a **London-pattern trowel** has one curved edge for cutting bricks, a skill that requires much practice to perfect. The blade's other edge is straight, for picking up mortar. This type of trowel is made in right- and left-handed versions, so buy the correct one. A right-handed trowel has its curved edge on the right when you point it away from you.

A **Canadian-pattern trowel** is symmetrical, enabling both left- and right-handed people to use it.

Pointing trowel

The blade of a pointing trowel is no more than 3 to 4 inches long, designed for repairing or shaping mortar joints between bricks.

Pointer

A pointer is shaped for making 'V' or concave joints between bricks. The narrow blade is dragged along the mortar joint and the curved front end is used to shape the verticals.

Frenchman

A Frenchman is a specialized tool for cutting excess mortar away from brickwork jointing. You can make one by heating and bending an old table knife.

Continental-pattern trowels

Using a pointing tray

A pointing tray makes the filling of mortar joints very easy. Place the flat lip of the tray just under a horizontal joint and scrape the mortar into place with a jointer. Turn the tray around and push mortar into vertical joints through the gap between the raised sides.

• **Essential tools**
Brick trowel
Pointing trowel
Plasterer's trowel
Mortar board
Hawk
Level
Try square
Plumb line

75

Wooden float
A wooden float is for applying and smoothing stucco and concrete to a fine, attractive texture. The more expensive ones have detachable handles so that their wooden blades can be replaced when they wear. But the amateur is unlikely to use a float often enough to justify the cost of buying one.

Plasterer's trowel
A plasterer's trowel is a steel float for applying plaster and stucco to walls. It is also dampened and used for "polishing," stroking the surface of the material when it has firmed up. Some builders prefer to apply stucco with a heavy trowel and finish it with a more flexible blade, but one has to be quite skilled to exploit such subtle differences.

DRILLS
A powerful electric drill is invaluable to a builder, but a hand brace is useful when you have to bore holes outdoors or in attics and cellars that lack convenient electric sockets.

Power drill
Buy a power drill, a range of twist drills and some spade or power-bore bits for drilling lumber. Make sure that the tool has a percussion or hammer action for drilling masonry. For masonry you need special drill bits tipped with tungsten carbide. The smaller ones are matched to the size of standard wall plugs, though there are much larger ones with reduced shanks that can be used in a standard power-drill chuck. The larger bits are expensive, so rent them when you need them. Percussion bits are even tougher than masonry bits, with shatterproof tips.

Brace and bit
A brace and bit is the ideal hand tool for drilling large holes in lumber, and when fitted with a screwdriver bit, it gives good leverage for driving or extracting large woodscrews.

Drilling masonry for wall plugs
Set the drill for low speed and hammer action, and wrap tape around the bit to mark the depth to be drilled. Allow for slightly more depth than the length of the plug, as dust will pack down into the hole when you insert it. Drill the hole in stages.

Protect floor coverings and paintwork from falling dust by taping a paper bag under the position of the hole before you start drilling.

• Essential tools
Straightedge
Tape measure
Claw hammer
Light sledgehammer
Panel saw
Tenon saw
Hacksaw
Padsaw
Power drill
Masonry bits
Brace and bit

BOARDS FOR CARRYING MORTAR OR PLASTER
Any convenient-sized sheet of ½- or ¾-inch exterior-grade plywood can be used as a mixing board for plaster or mortar. A panel about 3 feet square is ideal, and a smaller spotboard, about 2 feet square, is convenient for carrying the material to the actual work site. In either case, screw some wood strips to the undersides of the boards to make them easier to lift and carry. Make a small, lightweight hawk for carrying pointing mortar or plaster by nailing a single strip underneath a plywood board so that you can plug a handle into it.

A homemade hawk

HAMMERS
Very few hammers are needed on a building site.

Claw hammer
Choose a strong claw hammer for building wooden stud partitions, nailing floorboards, making door and window frames and putting up fencing.

Light sledgehammer
A light sledgehammer is used for driving cold chisels and for various demolition jobs. It is also useful for driving large masonry nails into walls.

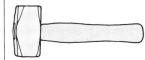

Sledgehammer
Rent a big sledgehammer if you have to break up concrete or paving. It's also the best tool for driving stakes or fence posts into the ground, though you can make do with a light sledge if the ground is not too hard.

Mallet
A carpenter's wooden mallet is the proper tool for driving wood chisels, but you can use a hammer if the chisels have impact-resistant plastic handles.

SAWS
Every builder needs a range of handsaws, but consider renting a power saw when you have to cut a lot of heavy structural timbers, and especially if you plan to rip floorboards down to width, a very tiring job when done by hand.

There are special power saws for cutting metal, and even for sawing through masonry.

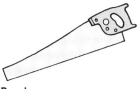

Panel saw
All kinds of man-made building boards are used in house construction, so buy a good panel saw—useful also for cutting large structural timbers to the required lengths.

Tenon saw
A tenon saw accurately cuts wall studs, floorboards, paneling and joints. Metal stiffening along the top of the blade keeps it rigid and less likely to go off line.

Padsaw
Also called a keyhole saw, this small saw has a narrow tapered blade for cutting holes in wood.

Coping saw
A coping saw has a frame that holds a fairly coarse but very narrow blade under tension for cutting curves in wood.

Floorboard saw
If you pry a floorboard above its neighbors you can cut across it with an ordinary tenon saw. But a floorboard saw's curved cutting edge makes it easier to avoid damaging the board on either side.

Hacksaw
The hardened-steel blades of a hacksaw have fine teeth for cutting metal. Use one to cut steel concrete-reinforcing rods or small pieces of sheet metal.

Sheet saw
A hacksaw's frame makes it unsuitable for cutting large sheets of metal. For that job, bolt a hacksaw blade to the edge of the flat blade of a sheet saw, which will also cut corrugated plastic sheeting and roofing slates.

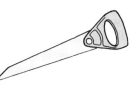

Universal saw
A universal or general-purpose saw is designed to cut wood, metal, plastics and building boards. Its short frameless blade has a low-friction coating and is stiff enough to make straight cuts without wandering. The handle can be set at various angles. The saw is particularly useful for cutting secondhand lumber, which may contain nails or screws that would blunt an ordinary saw.

Masonry saw
A masonry saw looks much like a wood handsaw but its tungsten-carbide teeth cut brick, concrete blocks and stone.

POWER SAWS
A *circular saw* will accurately rip lumber or man-made boards down to size. As well as doing away with the effort of hand-sawing large timbers, a sharp power saw produces such a clean cut that there is often no need for planing afterwards.

A *power jigsaw* cuts curves in lumber and sheet materials but is also useful for cutting holes in fixed wall panels and sawing through floorboards so as to lift them.

A *reciprocating saw* is a two-handed power saw with a long pointed blade, powerful enough to cut through heavy timber sections and even through a complete stud partition, panels and all.

GLAZIER'S TOOLS

Glass is such a hard and brittle material that it can be worked only with specialized tools.

Glass cutter
A glass cutter doesn't really cut glass but scores a line in it. The scoring is done by a tiny hardened-steel wheel or a chip of industrial diamond mounted in the penlike holder. The glass will break along the scored line when pressure is applied to it.

Beam compass cutter
A beam compass cutter is for scoring circles on glass—when, for example, you need a round hole in a window pane to fit a ventilator. The cutting wheel is mounted at the end of an adjustable beam that turns on a center pivot which is fixed to the glass by suction.

Spear-point glass drill
A glass drill has a flat spearhead-shaped tip of tungsten-steel shaft. The shape of the tip reduces friction that would otherwise crack the glass, but it needs lubricating with oil, paraffin or water during drilling.

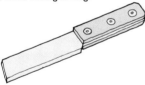

Hacking knife
A hacking knife has a heavy steel blade for chipping old putty out of window rabbets so as to remove the glass. Place its point between the putty and the frame and tap its thickened back with a hammer.

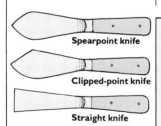

Spearpoint knife

Clipped-point knife

Straight knife

Putty knife
The blunt blade of a putty knife is for shaping and smoothing fresh putty. You can choose between spearpoint, clipped-point and straight blades according to your personal preference.

CHISELS

As well as chisels for cutting and paring wood joints, you will need some special ones for masonry work.

Cold chisel
Cold chisels are made from solid steel hexagonal-section rod. They are primarily for cutting metal bars and chopping the heads off rivets, but a builder will use one for cutting a chase in plaster and brickwork or chopping out old brick pointing.

Slip a plastic safety sleeve over the chisel to protect your hand from a misplaced blow with the sledgehammer.

Plugging chisel
A plugging chisel has a flat narrow bit (tip) for cutting out old pointing. It's worth renting one if you have a large area of brickwork to repoint.

Bricklayer's chisel
The wide bit of a bricklayer's chisel is for cutting bricks and concrete blocks. It's also useful for levering up floorboards.

WORK GLOVES

Wear strong work gloves whenever you carry paving stones, concrete blocks or rough lumber. Ordinary gardening gloves are better than none but won't last long on a building site. The best work gloves have leather palms and fingers, though you may prefer a pair with ventilated backs for comfort in hot weather.

DIGGING TOOLS

Much building work requires some kind of digging—for laying strip foundations and concrete pads, sinking rows of postholes and so on. You may already have the essential tools in your garden shed; others you can rent.

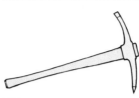

Pickaxe
Use a medium-weight pickaxe to break up heavily compacted soil, especially if it contains a lot of buried rubble.

Mattlock
The wide blade of a mattock is ideal for breaking up heavy clay soil, and it's better than an ordinary pickaxe for ground that's riddled with tree roots.

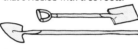

Spade
Buy a good-quality spade for excavating soil and mixing concrete. One with a stainless-steel blade is best, but alloy steel will last fairly well if it is looked after. For strength choose a D-shaped handle whose hardwood shaft has been split and riveted with metal plates to the crosspiece, and make sure that the shaft socket and blade are forged in one piece.

Square blades seem to be the most popular, though some builders prefer a round-mouth spade with a long pole handle for digging deep trenches and holes.

Shovel
You can use a spade for mixing and placing concrete or mortar, but the raised edges of a shovel retain it better.

Garden rake
Use an ordinary garden rake to spread gravel or level wet concrete, but be sure to wash it before any concrete sets on it.

Posthole auger
Rent a posthole auger to sink narrow holes for fence and gate posts by driving it into the ground like a corkscrew and pulling out plugs of earth.

Wheelbarrow
The average garden wheelbarrow is not really strong enough for work on building sites, which entails carrying heavy loads of wet concrete and rubble. Unless the tubular underframe is rigidly strutted, the barrow's thin metal body will distort and perhaps spill its load as you cross rough ground. Check, too, that the axle is fixed securely. Cheap wheelbarrows often lose their wheels when their loads are being tipped into excavations.

SCREWDRIVERS

One's choice of screwdrivers is a personal matter, and most people accumulate a collection of types and sizes over the years.

Cabinet screwdriver
Buy at least one large flat-tip screwdriver. The fixed variety is quite adequate but a pump-action one, which drives large screws very quickly, is useful when you assemble big wooden building structures.

Phillips-head screwdriver
Choose the size and type of Phillips-head screwdriver to suit the work at hand. There is no most useful size as the driver must fit the screw slots exactly.

PLANES

Your choice of planes depends on the kind of joinery you plan to do. Sophisticated framing may call for molding or grooving planes, but most woodwork needs only skimming to leave a fairly smooth finish.

Jack plane
A medium-size bench plane, the jack plane, is the best general-purpose tool.

ADDITIONAL BUILDER'S TOOLS
The following tools would be a useful addition to a builder's tool kit, especially when carrying out major repairs and improvements.

Crowbar
A crowbar, or wrecking bar, is for demolishing timber framework. Force the flat tip between components and use the leverage of the long shaft to pry them apart. Choose a bar that has a claw at one end for removing large nails.

- **Essential tools**
  Glass cutter
  Putty knife
  Cold chisel
  Bricklayer's chisel
  Spade
  Shovel
  Rake
  Wheelbarrow
  Cabinet screwdriver
  Phillips-head screwdriver
  Jack plane

B

Batt
A short, cut length of fiberglass or mineral-fiber insulant.

Batten
A narrow strip of wood.

Bridging
See *cross-braces*.

C

Casing
The wooden molding around a door opening.

Chamfer
A narrow, flat surface on the edge of a piece of wood—normally at an angle of 45 degrees to adjacent surfaces; *or*, to plane the angled surface.

Chase
A groove cut in masonry or plaster to accept pipework or an electrical cable; *or*, to cut such a groove.

Cornice
The continuous horizontal molding between walls and ceiling.

Counterbore
To cut a hole that allows the head of a bolt or screw to lie below a surface; *or*, the hole itself.

Countersink
To cut a tapered recess that allows the head of a screw to lie flush with a surface; *or*, the tapered recess itself.

Cripple
A short piece of *stud* installed vertically above a door jamb.

Cross-braces
Diagonal wooden or metal braces nailed between floor joists to prevent twisting; also called bridging; *or*, short horizontal wooden members nailed between studs to stiffen them.

D

Dado
A groove cut into a piece of wood, running across the grain.

Dowel
A short, round wooden rod used to join two pieces of wood.

F

Fascia board
A strip of wood that covers the ends of rafters and to which external guttering is fixed.

Flashing
A weatherproof junction between a roof and a wall or chimney, or between one roof and another.

Footing
A narrow concrete foundation for a wall.

Furring strips
Parallel strips of wood fixed to a wall or ceiling to provide a framework for attaching panels.

G

Galvanized
Covered with a protective coating of zinc.

Grounds
Strips of wood fixed to a wall to provide nail-fixing points for baseboards and door casings.

H

Header
The top horizontal member of a wooden frame.

Horns
Extended door or window *stiles* designed to protect the corners from damage while in storage.

J

Jamb
The vertical side member of a door or window frame; *or*, the frame as a whole.

Joist
A horizontal wooden or metal beam used to support a structure such as a floor, ceiling, or wall.

K

Kerf
The groove cut by a saw.

Key
To abrade or incise a surface to provide a better grip when gluing something to it.

L

Lath and plaster
A method of finishing a stud-framed wall or ceiling in which narrow strips of wood are nailed to the *studs* or *joists* to provide a supporting framework for plaster.

Lintel
A horizontal beam used to support the wall over a door or window opening.

M

Miter
A joint formed between two pieces of wood by cutting bevels of equal angles at the ends of each piece; *or*, to cut such a joint.

Mortise
A rectangular recess cut in timber to receive a matching tongue, or *tenon*.

Mullion
A vertical dividing member of a window frame.

Muntin
A central vertical member of a panel door.

N

Needle
A stout wooden beam used with props to support the section of a wall above an opening prior to the installation of a *rolled-steel joist* or a *lintel*.

P

Party wall
The wall between two houses, over which each of the adjoining owners has equal rights.

Pilot hole
A small-diameter hole drilled prior to the insertion of a woodscrew to serve as a guide for the screw's thread.

Pinch rod
A wooden *batten* used to gauge the width of a door casing.

Plate
The top horizontal member of a *stud partition*.

Purlin
A horizontal beam that provides intermediate support for *rafters* or sheet roofing.

R

Rabbet
A stepped recess along the edge of a workpiece, usually as part of a joint; *or*, to cut such recesses.

Rafter
One of a set of parallel sloping beams that form the main structural element of a roof.

Reveal
The vertical side of an opening in a wall.

Rolled-steel joist
A steel beam usually with a cross section in the form of a letter I.

S

Sash
The openable part of a window.

Screed batten
A thin strip of wood fixed to a surface to act as a thickness and leveling guide when applying plaster; also called a screed.

Scribe
To copy the profile of a surface on the edge of sheet material that is to be butted against the surface; *or*, to mark a line with a pointed tool.

Sheathing
The outer covering of a stud-framed wall over which wall siding is installed; *or*, the outer layer of insulation surrounding an electrical cable.

Sill
The lowest horizontal member of a *stud partition; or*, the lowest horizontal member of a door or window frame.

Sleeper wall
A low masonry wall used as an intermediate support for ground-floor *joists*.

Soffit
The underside of a part of a building, such as the eaves or an archway.

Sole
Another name for a stud-partition *sill; or*, a wooden member used as a base to level a stud-framed load-bearing wall.

Stile
A vertical side member of a door or window *sash*.

Stud partition
An interior stud-framed dividing wall.

Stud
A vertical member of a stud-framed wall.

T

Tenon
A projecting tongue on the end of a piece of wood that fits in a corresponding *mortise*.

Transom
A horizontal dividing member of a window frame.

U

Undercoat
A layer of paint used to obliterate the color of a primer and to build a protective body of paint prior to the application of a top coat.

V

Vapor barrier
A layer of impervious material that prevents the passage of moisture.

W

Wall plate
A horizontal timber member placed along the top of a wall to support *joists* and to spread their load.

Wall tie
A strip of metal or bent wire used to bind sections of masonry together.